IN THE

RAISING SONS TO BE MEN OF UNYIELDING

CONVICTION IN A CULTURE OF CONFUSION

OF IT

IN THE

RAISING SONS TO BE MEN OF UNYIELDING

CONVICTION IN A CULTURE OF CONFUSION

OF IT

JASON CRUISE

SHILOH RUN  PRESS

An Imprint of Barbour Publishing, Inc.

Published by Shiloh Run Press, an imprint of Barbour Publishing, Inc., 1810 Barbour Drive, Uhrichsville, Ohio 44683, www.shilohrunpress.com

Our mission is to inspire the world with the life-changing message of the Bible.

 Member of the
Evangelical Christian
Publishers Association

Printed in the United States of America.

To my dad, Larry Cruise.
You have been the constant force behind my every step. Your work ethic
pushed me to what I know about sacrifice to get ahead. Your spoken love
and approval have covered me in the risks I've taken through the years.
Your presence has never been away from me. I am forever indebted.

CONTENTS

DIVIDED LOYALTIES

A man must choose sides.

Every dad must choose sides, but few seem able to do it.

Divided loyalty. That's where many men get lost in raising sons.

Raising boys will straight kill a man if he isn't sure where his loyalty lies.

I knew before we had our first son that I was going to have to pick a path. There was no dotted yellow line splitting this path either. It was a one-way domain, and just as American poet Robert Frost observed, even I could see that few around me were choosing it:

> *Two roads diverged in a wood, and I,*
> *I took the one less traveled by,*
> *And that has made all the difference.*[1]

There were a few dads choosing, but few indeed. And in the end, I didn't care if I had to walk the path alone. I knew before we had our first son that modern culture offered me nothing—*nothing*—that I wanted my sons to possess.

I have two sons: Cole and Tucker.

I knew even before I met them that they deserved everything I have to offer to prepare them for manhood. Even if I have to walk the path alone.

DUPED

If you're just now starting this journey of biblical manhood—especially parenting from the context of biblical manhood—know that it is not going to be easy. Sure, you've heard it said many times, but I'm telling you, friend, it's true.

I'm currently in my second decade of raising boys; one is

about to become a teenager, and the other isn't far behind. I can promise you that you, like me, are going to wonder, *Am I doing this right?*

Don't worry. Your parents wondered the same thing. I'd only been a dad for a few days when I became aware that my mom and dad had made things up on the fly.

That's right. Parents often make things up and sell them to their kids as concrete, scientific, and established truth on how the world works. I've done it too many times to count!

My mama is going to read this. So is my daddy. And I'm telling everyone, including them, that parents are the ultimate con artists. Many times when we're in a parental bind, my wife, Michelle, and I both launch the question, "Is this the best decision?"

I was a dad for only about six minutes when I realized that society had done me wrong. I needed both an offensive—and a defensive—playbook for fatherhood, scripted with elaborate contingency plans that included pictures. Lots and lots of pictures. And instructional video links too. Yet I had nothing of the kind. Unfortunately, there is no playbook for parenting.

With that in mind, know that my intention is not to toss out evangelical antidotes on all that is wrong with raising boys in this tolerant modern era. A man could spend a career grasping at such a Solomon's wind. And to be quite candid, I don't have the brainpower to be that clever.

I'D BE LYING IF I DENIED IT

In fact, this was a mind-bending book for me to write.

Too many times in recent days, just after duck season ended and the deadline for this book was on the horizon, my mind drifted to the terror of this assumption: *People are going to think I'm an arrogant jerk when they read this. Seriously, who has the gall to put out content on how to parent kids?*

Understand that I wasn't raised a philosopher, and I don't consider myself to be one. I did not come from academia, although there is nothing wrong with that. I came from blue-collar roots. My daddy drove a used Chevy truck and owned a small business: an outdoors store, where he opened the doors every morning at 5 a.m.

My family was a classic American family. Mama worked. Daddy worked. Mama cooked dinner every night. Dad threw a baseball with me in the yard. Dad coached my baseball teams and took me hunting and fishing. And such was life.

So if you think I had a plan for raising children all neatly wrapped up and ready to go when my first son was born, well, you'd be quite mistaken. Nevertheless, I wasn't left without any help. I had learned a lot about being a dad, and I was more prepared than I realized at the time.

THEY CALL IT MODELING

My mom and dad supported my educational journey. They were

too busy trying to put food on the table to further their own education, and like all parents, they wanted better options for their son.

So off to college I went, and from there on to graduate school. It was in the work of academia where I first encountered the word *modeling*. Modeling would describe much of how I learned about being a dad—my dad was a master at it. But if you asked my dad today about how he modeled manhood for me, he'd probably look at you with a humble, confused grin.

I'm forever stopping to coach my boys. I'm sure they get weary from my edicts, but it's their lot in life, I suppose. Yes, I'll stop at just about anything and take the podium if I think there's a life lesson to be learned. My dad, on the other hand, didn't explain a ton of things to me. He just lived as an example before me.

I have forever been close to my dad, and we communicated very well, but men in those days just didn't think like the dads of today. There weren't as many books and seminars, and no podcasts and blogs flooding a man with an artesian well of insight on how to raise kids. No, in those days men worked and did the best they could do.

WATCH

Watch. That's what I did. I noticed how my dad handled things. I listened when he talked business. I took notice of the way he shook a man's hand. I stood in awe at how he never backed down, not a single inch, from a customer who tried to intimidate him. I logged information on the ways he approached people, debt, hunting, and sports.

I could see that my dad wasn't listening to the cultural pressure plaguing many parents in those days. And above all else, I could see that my dad had convictions—convictions that drove his actions.

That is the point: *a man must choose sides.* A man must choose the path. A man must pick the ideals and values that he will instill in his children.

If you don't choose—if you're passive—culture will choose your children's ideals and values. Your children's minds and hearts are open ground. If you don't lead them toward holy truth, culture will capture them—without remorse. And their enemy, the devil, will ensure that their hearts don't stay open long.

Your loyalty to choosing God's authority over how you parent must be concrete.

What path have you chosen?

THE JUDGMENT DAY
OF POPULAR OPINION

I can picture it now.

I write this book, and it lands me on center stage. Oh, not with fat stacks of money and fame, but with cultural awe and wonder: I'm seen as a sort of caveman.

I can see it so clearly. I'm on a nationally syndicated morning show, and the hosts are looking at me like I'm some evangelical, two-headed beast with no teeth from the remote canyons of the northeastern Georgia mountains. Banjo music is playing in the background.

"Who knew these people still existed out there?" is the sound bite leading into the live televised segment. The audience is staring at me with intrigue, as if I'm a zoo-like creature, while the host is taking verbal jabs at my values.

It's dramatic, I know. And I also know that I'm not alone in how I view today's pop culture trends—though it feels like it at times. Nevertheless, many modern trendsetters will view me as if I am a caveman.

CULTURAL WARFARE

When I thought about writing this book, it crossed my mind more than once that perhaps the wisest route would be to write a creative concoction with a nod to James Dobson and John Eldredge, and perhaps a little Steve Chapman. Maybe I should surrender to this thought and find a way to call it my own savvy, southern work on how to raise a boy who has true grit, a son with an inner warrior and a heart for God.

It's been said that the cheapest form of flattery is imitation, so yeah, a small dose of plagiarism could be my best option. Right?

Even though these great men have written from decades of experience, the reality that our rapidly changing culture demands still more needs to be said caused me to press forward with this project.

We can attest that the things Dobson wrote about in *Bringing Up Boys*, the issues boys deal with psychologically and physiologically, are at least somewhat consistent from generation to generation.

When Eldredge wrote *Wild at Heart*, it struck at the core DNA of every man, regardless of his era of birth. A man was created with a need for adventure on many levels, and Eldredge conveyed that truth well.

When Chapman wrote *10 Ways to Prepare Your Son for Life*,

again, those were, and are to this day, timeless bedrock principles.

Ever since I've become a parent, however, culture has shifted furiously and quickly, with seemingly no signs of stopping. And that compels me to speak up.

Culture has morphed into what feels akin to a toxic *Matrix* plot come to real life. You'd have to be locked in a dungeon not to have noticed. Political correctness interwoven with heretical views of tolerance have eroded the country I now live in to the point that I hardly recognize the nation of my birth.

We are in a culture that is mixed up, turned around, and lost. And here we are as dads, having to raise boys in a culture that literally wants to debate anatomy and can't seem to agree on what a boy is by definition!

This means every dad had better be ready, and ready for today. Every dad needs a plan; and while my insights on fatherhood are far from perfect, they are at least on time.

The hearts and minds of my boys are not for sale. I am the gatekeeper of their hearts and minds, and I will not let their futures be determined by the highest bidder.

THE QUESTION YOU MUST ANSWER

This *choosing of sides* I've been hinting at to this point is found in the idea of authority.

You're going to have to choose: Who is the authority governing how you raise your sons? Who is the authority that gets the right to tell *you* what to believe about fatherhood?

A man cannot raise boys with a God-designed intention and yet cater to divided loyalties. There's just too much on the line for you to try and navigate fatherhood absent of convictions.

You must choose your source of authority; that is, you must choose *who* gets the right to structure your worldview.

And look, it's not as easy as it sounds.

All my life I've seen those bumper stickers. You've seen them too: THE BIBLE SAYS IT. I BELIEVE IT. THAT SETTLES IT.

That is all very true, but just because the Bible says it doesn't mean evangelicals abide by it.

We live in a world wrought by seemingly mundane decisions. Many of those decisions we make in daily quiet moments, but it is in the quiet moments when a divided will, a divided loyalty, shows up most.

Jesus had quite a bit to say about a divided life. He knew culture would push and sway His followers. Look at the haunting clarity in Luke's gospel. Read it slowly and let it sink deep:

> *"I say to you, My friends, do not be afraid of those who kill the body and after that have no more that they can do. But I will warn you whom to fear: fear the One who, after He has killed, has authority to cast into hell; yes, I tell you, fear Him!"*
> LUKE 12:4–5

There's intensity there, am I right? I can hear it in Jesus' voice. I can almost see it in His eyes.

A man must choose who gets to be his boss, and we'd all better fear the One worth fearing.

THE PHILOSOPHER IN YOU

Each of us has a worldview. You cannot escape it. Your worldview sticks to you whether or not you want it to.

How you look at the world is much like looking through a pair of glasses. And those glasses were put together through life experiences, things your parents did or didn't do, successes, songs, sermons, victories and defeats, and the lessons those moments taught you. Those internal glasses you wear, and through which you look at life, were part made up by you and part passed on to you from others.

The problem for many evangelicals is that their worldview is like a stew mixed with a little of Grandma's wisdom, lessons from their own parents, notes taken from their favorite movies on how life and love work, limited theological understanding, and their favorite Christian songs on the radio. We gather belief systems from a wide range of life experiences.

My point is this: nearly every Christian I know, including me, carries an infected worldview. What else could possibly explain the wide gap we often see in Christian behavior and Christian theology?

Much of what you believe was handed down to you. And when you aren't the sole owner of your theology, life gets divided. Jesus had a lot to say about that too.

> *The Pharisees and some of the scribes gathered around Him when they had come from Jerusalem, and had seen that some of His disciples were eating their bread with impure hands, that is, unwashed. (For the Pharisees and all the Jews do not eat unless they carefully wash their hands, thus observing the traditions of the elders; and when they come from the market place, they do not eat unless they cleanse themselves; and there are many other things which they have received in order to observe, such as the washing of cups and pitchers and copper pots.)*
>
> *The Pharisees and the scribes asked Him, "Why do Your disciples not walk according to the tradition of the elders, but eat their bread with impure hands?"*
>
> *And He said to them, "Rightly did Isaiah prophesy of you hypocrites, as it is written:*
> *'This people honors Me with their lips,*
> *But their heart is far away from Me.*
> *But in vain do they worship Me,*
> *Teaching as doctrines the precepts of men.'*
> *Neglecting the commandment of God, you hold to the tradition of men."*
> MARK 7:1–8

A person's theology comes from tradition as much as it does from organic truth. We all have that going on inside of us, and God has to get it out of us.

When your theology about raising kids—theology about anything, for that matter—is taken from what your parents told you to believe and what your preacher told you to believe and what your youth minister told you to believe, you're going to find yourself smack in the middle of a divided life because you don't actually *own* the theology driving your life.

You're just borrowing it.

When your borrowed theology drives your life, don't expect it to hold up under pressure. And when culture leans hard on you, don't expect borrowed theology to give you peace or direction.

LEANING—HARD

There's a leadership axiom that I love because it just makes sense.

If you've read any of my books, or if you get my "Man Minute" devotionals that are delivered every Monday, or if you've followed me on social media for any amount of time, you've likely known me to use this simple illustration. It's an old leadership principle that just works, and it comes in the form of a question:

How do you turn a large battleship?
Constant pressure on a small rudder.

Pop culture thinking seeps into your worldview no matter

how much spiritual caulk you place around your evangelical heart. No person is completely immune from cultural pressures. That doesn't excuse behavior, but don't think for a second that culture doesn't play a role in spiritual formation.

Every single day you're told by liberal media that "normal" people are tolerant. Every day you're told by liberal media that "normal" people wouldn't dare judge sexual deviancy, even when it is clearly defined by scripture. Every day you're told by liberal media which clothes are considered acceptable to wear. Every day you're being told how to live, how to think, and what's proper and acceptable about how to live and how to think.

Every day—*every single day*—society leans on you, putting constant pressure on the small rudder of your heart and mind.

Now that we have the most biblically illiterate society in human history, you can see where this is going.

And I'm not even talking about non-Christians. I expect non-believers to act like nonbelievers. I'm talking about churchgoers.

When you take biblical illiteracy among Christians and couple it with a society that stays glued to a smartphone—well, should we expect anything less than what we have now?

HOW I OVERCAME POP CULTURE FATHERHOOD

It's strange to say it, because it sounds completely cavalier and out of touch; however, the truth is, I never cared about outside opinions when it came to how I was going to raise my children.

I have never ever honestly cared at all about what people think about me in terms of how I am raising my boys. In fact, to say that may even seem hypocritical. Earlier I went into great detail about how I was concerned at the outset of this project that people might think I consider myself the foremost authority on raising boys—that I'm a know-it-all.

However, when it comes to how others see me as a father, or the methods and ideologies I employ in raising my boys, what others might think doesn't enter my thinking.

Any person who says, "I just don't care what anyone thinks of me" is lying to themselves. We all have at least a few people whose opinions *really do* matter to us, at least on some level.

My chosen path for how I'm raising boys is a place where I've resolved to be quite independent and immune from public perception.

There's a very real, clear reason for why I feel that way: *God's judgment.*

CHOSEN

While you and I have likely never met, we do have at least one brutal reality in common: we are both going to die, and we will both individually stand before God.

Do you know whom I will not be standing before on that day?

As nice as she may be, I will not stand before Oprah for an account on how I lived my life.

I will not be standing before Jimmy Fallon. Or Jimmy Kimmel. I will not stand before Brad Pitt. Or Sean Penn. Or Tucker Carlson. Or Rush Limbaugh. Or Jerry Seinfeld. Or Matt Lauer. Or Anderson Cooper.

I will not stand before congressmen who tell me what is or is not the lawful and right thing to do in today's world.

I will not stand before George W. Bush, Barack Obama, or Donald Trump.

I will not stand before my employer.

I will not stand before my very own dad and his idea of how I did with raising his two grandsons.

When I die, I'll be standing before a holy God.

And that's why I've chosen to bow to His authority, found in His Word, on how I raise my boys. That includes bowing to the totality of His authority—not just the parts of His Word that I like most and that fit my worldview or desires. I've chosen to submit myself, and the way I raise my boys, to the One who will hold my soul and spirit accountable.

And you too must choose whose authority you will bow to.

REDEFINING THE GOAL

My goal has never been to be my sons' best friend.

Rather, my goal has forever been to raise boys with this one simple foundation: biblical manhood. I want my boys to own for themselves what it means to understand, embody, and walk out biblical manhood of the most rugged sort. Not contrived. Not cowboyed up. Not machismo. I want them to own what it means to be a man—and to be a man of God—on every level.

I knew from the beginning that I could not afford divided loyalties in terms of whom I was trying to please in raising my boys. This means that my goal has never been to operate in the shallow end of the patriarchal pool, merely wanting to be my sons' friend.

I suppose that may sound harsh at first take. I can see how someone might look at me and say, "Why? Why would you not want to be your son's go-to guy, his best of friends?"

It isn't that I wouldn't love that to be the outcome, but it isn't my goal. I cannot afford for "best friend status" to be the target of my journey with Cole or Tucker.

The answer to "Why?" comes down to math. Calculate it in your head, and eventually you'll see it when the math finally comes together.

I have a real-life story that might give some insight into my feelings on this issue, and perhaps it will help you better understand my approach.

A SEEMINGLY ORDINARY LUNCH

I try to have lunch every day with a man in my circle of influence. It was a habit I started early in ministry when I was first pastoring churches. I daresay that few things I've ever done have been as important and lasting as lunch. I'm not joking.

I started my career in ministry when I was seventeen years old. After a few years of experimenting in various roles within church ministry, it became apparent to me that my wheelhouse, my area of strength, was in any form of ministry that centered around men.

That made sense to me. I was always better at reaching men. I'm not a woman. I don't think like a woman. I don't want to think like a woman. And so I try not to overthink it.

Ministry comes in many forms, but no matter what form of ministry we are called to, we are called to the care of souls. Ministry is, in many aspects, geared toward being a soul coach. And I seem to coach the souls of men the best.

I learned quickly that a man must eat. I've never met a man

who doesn't like to eat. And when you're a soul coach who desires to get into the lives of men and point them toward the deeper things of being a Jesus follower, lunch is a great way to get it done.

Lunch is single-handedly the most effective way I've ever been able to access the hearts of men. And that includes executives, mechanics, plumbers, songwriters, bankers, and any other man you can imagine. Lunch works, because while at lunch, men do not feel as if they are interrupting their workflow to spend time with you.

And so lunch has been the best tool in my soul toolbox.

Years ago I found myself having lunch with a friend who was a new dad and a very intelligent businessman. Michelle and I were still not yet quite to the point of having children, but my buddy had one son and another on the way.

We were dining at a Cracker Barrel. A glass of iced tea sat in front of me, a ring of condensation forming at the base. And a half-eaten piece of corn bread rested on a small plate, substantiating the franchise's attempt to give their customers Mama's cooking on a freeway exit ramp. It was during this seemingly ordinary lunch that our conversation turned to raising children.

ON THROWIN' A FIT

My friend has a job that requires a lot of office time and long hours. He makes a boatload of money too. He had managed, however, to curb those insane work hours once kids entered the narrative. I admired him for that because he was in an elevated position with a recognized brand.

His son, by my amateur estimation, was a normal rowdy and demanding three-year-old boy. At times he was seemingly disrespectful—more than just a three-year-old's attitude that we all know too well as parents. This kid had a snarl about him, which I really didn't know what to make of, since after all, he was only three.

My friend began to talk about a rage his son threw the night before at suppertime. Evidently the boy wasn't happy about something and just wouldn't settle down—acting rude to his mama, throwing some food, fake crying, all the drama kids attempt in that stage of life when trying to get their way. He was, as we say in the South, "throwin' a fit."

My friend's response as a dad to the situation had me thinking about the responsibility of raising children for several days after the lunch was over.

He said, "You know, by the time I get home, I only get about three hours a night with him. And so I'm thinking, *If I spank him, it's going to ruin the meal, and he's going to be upset all evening.* So, do you just move on and try and get through it, or what? I don't get a ton of time with him to begin with, you know? So I just moved on with the meal."

BE CAREFUL BEFORE YOU SAY IT

It's easy to say what you would do in that moment.

Think about how often you say the words, "I'll tell you what I'd do. . . ." We're all guilty of it. Most every person walking the planet truly believes they know how they would handle any given situation.

With several decades of life on planet Earth under my belt now, and especially a decade more on this side of being a dad, I can tell you this: you often don't have a clue what you'd do in any situation.

You *hope* you know what you'd do.

You have a fairly decent *guess* about what you'd do, but be careful before you say, "I'll tell you what I'd do," because you might just find yourself embarrassed in the not-so-distant future.

In light of my friend's choice to *move on* with dinner, it was easy for me to spell out what I'd do in such a moment.

I didn't have fit-throwin' kids yet. I wasn't exhausted from a day's work in the corporate sector, only to come home and see real drama just beginning to unfold. I wasn't mentally exhausted from the second night of arguing with my wife because we were both sleep deprived and I was wanting dinner while she was hungry for any conversation that didn't involve the finer mechanics of Legos and sippy cups.

All of that—*all of it*—culminates in that seemingly ordinary, mundane, daily moment where you just want to do what my friend said he had done: "move on and try and get through it."

So now do the math. Play out that scenario fifteen years from now. After fifteen years of just trying to get through it and be your son's best friend, what are you left with?

When you try and be your son's best friend, it doesn't seem that bad. Not in the moment. When you are best friends, well, you're willing to let your best buddy break the rules.

The brutal reality is this: if you let him break your standards when he's six, he's going to break your heart when he's sixteen.

Even when the boundaries and standards seem so incredibly inconsequential as throwing a tantrum on a Tuesday evening at suppertime while screaming at his mama because he doesn't like the situation he's in at the moment—that moment, my dear brother, is huge—monumental.

It turns out that life is just one moment after another. String enough of those moments together, and you've got yourself a story.

> **IF YOU LET HIM BREAK YOUR STANDARDS WHEN HE'S SIX, HE'S GOING TO BREAK YOUR HEART WHEN HE'S SIXTEEN**

IT'S FAST, AND IT'S NOT FAIR

You want to see pain?

I'll give a simple task, and you watch for yourself the type of response you get. I don't have the gift of prophecy, but I'll guarantee 100 percent that you get the same response.

Today find five people who have kids over the age of fifteen, and ask them this simple question: How fast did your kids growing up before your very eyes happen?

The look in their eyes will be nothing short of heavy.

They will struggle to find the exact words. Words will get in the way of their trying somehow to convince you of the harsh reality that you have mere moments—short, *short* windows of time before you realize they are not growing up; they are *grown*.

That's the tragic part of parenting that every parent cannot change and must accept.

Just a few days ago I was talking with a buddy of mine about the dad life. He and his wife are about to have their first child, a daughter, whom they are going to name Ava—a classy, timeless name. I haven't seen her yet, but she's going to be knock-out pretty. I just know it.

I can't remember the context of the entire conversation, but I do remember relaying to my friend that the only thing about raising children that I don't like—that I, in fact, despise—is how fast it happens.

Everyone tries their best to tell you how fast your kids are going to grow up, but until you witness it for yourself, you can't comprehend it.

I do remember saying, "They grow up so fast that it's painful. It's actually painful. It's almost not fair."

So my advice to you would be to do the math.

Play out these moments for what they really are—brief incidents that happen just before you wake up and notice that your son is moving out of the house and driving a car out of your driveway. Because, friend, it happens about that fast.

That's the hard lesson I've had to learn myself over the years of being in the thick of it raising boys. You must train your mind to understand how a single moment translates into your son's future development as a man.

It may look like a simple supper on a Tuesday before you go and watch Netflix.

Today it's slapping his fork down on the table because he wants to watch his favorite show. Tomorrow it's punching a hole in the drywall and cursing his mama because she's cramping his lifestyle with her household rules that tell him his room cannot be mired in filth.

And so I return to the premise of this seemingly harsh statement about raising children: my goal has never been to be my sons' best friend.

That's right. My sons deserve more.

CULTURE AND PLUMB LINES

I'm not a big fan of comparison.

You don't find comparison much in scripture, if you find it at all. Our culture today, however, is seemingly obsessed with comparison.

I fall into comparison traps all the time. I compare my net worth to someone else's, or I judge my ability to be a romantic lover to my wife by how I stack up against her friends' husbands who take their wives on cool vacation getaways that are posted on Facebook.

Almost thirty years of ministry has taught me that a man can never—and I mean *never*—compare his marriage to the marriages of other couples. I learned pretty quickly in my early days of pastoring churches that you never know what's going on behind closed doors.

Many men are great at showing those around them how deep and wide their walk with God is, only to live it completely different in everyday life, which no one sees but his wife and children.

I'm not a fan of comparison. Far too often the devil has used comparison against me. However, that doesn't mean I'm against standards of comparison altogether, for we do in fact have to compare ourselves against God's standards. He gives us dads a measurement not for the sake of comparison, but rather as a plumb line of sorts to hold us to plumb for the sake of longevity. That plumb line comes in the form of an Old Testament verse referred to as the Shema.

STRANGE WORD, SERIOUS WORLDVIEW

Shema (pronounced Shuh-MAH) is short for the first two words of Deuteronomy 6:4, which starts out with the commandment from God to His people to listen closely: "*Sh'ma Yisrael*," or "Hear, O Israel."

This is the holy God talking, not some baseball coach trying to get your attention at a pregame meeting. This is the God of the universe, and He's about to hand down some serious blueprints for constructing your life in ways that bring longevity and success—success not by the world's standards, but success by eternal standards.

I have a bad habit of skipping over verses of scripture when I encounter them in book form. That is, if an author lists a long passage, I often don't read it, and that's just a bad habit. So I'm asking you not to do that.

We are going to use this passage for a monumental framework of the conversation you and I are having, and I want you to get it into your bones. Found in Deuteronomy 6:4–7, it is no doubt the plumb line for fathers.

> *"Hear, O Israel! The LORD is our God, the LORD is one! You shall love the LORD your God with all your heart and with all your soul and with all your might. These words, which I am commanding you today, shall be on your heart. You shall teach them diligently to your sons and shall talk of them when you sit in your house and when you walk by the way and when you lie down and when you rise up."*

Jesus quoted this commandment, which is often referred to as the Great Commandment, to love the Lord your God with all your heart and with all your soul and with all your might.

Yet it is what follows that grabs me: I am to teach God's words to my sons.

This commandment is not just for me; it is my responsibility to instill God's commands in my family members so that they will be passed on to those who come along far after I'm gone. Lives are at stake.

Think about that.

This monumental passage handed down from the heart of God to His people was given to them as a community. At the heart of the Shema is the fundamental understanding that the people of God must be aligned in the same worldview.

Think about that.

Training their families to obey God's commands was critical to their survival—literally. Life and longevity hung in the balance. The people of God must possess a heart for God or everything breaks down.

An oft-quoted parental axiom says, "It takes a village to raise a child." This African proverb was made famous by Hillary Clinton, who wrote a book based on the premise. I get the fundamental idea: all of us have responsibility to create a culture where we look out for the best interests of the generations coming behind us. The problem, however, is that in today's culture our villages do not possess a biblical worldview. Moreover, divorce has ravaged our society. Now put those two problems together: evaporating biblical culture + divorce = ?

What happens when both the village *and* the fathers go missing?

OF ELEPHANTS, TESTOSTERONE, AND MISSING FATHERS

In the early 1980s, a strange story began to unfold in South Africa. Do a web search around Kruger National Park elephant relocation and you'll find it.

The leaders at Kruger National Park felt that there were too many elephants, and coincidentally a new park had emerged nearby named Pilanesberg. Plans were made to transport older bulls to Pilanesberg, but there were problems with the harnesses needed to transport the elephants one by one via helicopter. The harnesses could handle younger males and females; so instead, younger bulls were transported to the new park in Pilanesberg.

Not many months after the relocations, park officials began coming upon dead rhinoceroses. Immediately, poaching was suspected. Upon inspection, however, there were no bullet holes to be found on the mutilated bodies of the rhinos.[1]

After staging cameras throughout the park, leaders discovered the problem. The young elephant bulls had formed a gang and were murdering rhinos. Not only was it fascinating, but their acting out was extremely uncharacteristic of the nature of elephants. Elephants just didn't act like this. So the park managers moved a few of the bulls to other parks and even killed a few of the gang leaders. Still, it happened again.

Over the course of the next several years, officials found better harnessing options and moved several mature bulls to Pilanesberg. The chief among them was named Amarula. He was a beast of a bull elephant—massive in size and well into adulthood.

Almost immediately, younger bulls began to approach Amarula to pay homage. A few rank, young bulls did not pay homage, and he stomped them into submission without hesitation. With further research, scientists discovered that young bulls enter into their version of testosterone over time, and it is the herd bulls that keep this process in check. The herd bull literally tempers their growth. With the arrival of mature bulls, the killing stopped almost overnight.[2]

BACK TO THE PLUMB LINE

I completed my doctoral work specializing in men's ministry issues at Fuller Theological Seminary. Doctoral work is both highly specific and intense; and though master's level work tends to be specific, it involves a wider scope within the discipline of focus.

I completed my master's at a seminary in Texas called Southwestern. It was a historic place to study. I never really expected much from the history professors. I know—you don't have to say it. I was in my twenties, and the idea of sitting in a history class, especially one centered on antiquity, left me wondering if root canal surgery would be preferable.

I was proven wrong time and again.

It was during my master's work that I had the honor of sitting under the teaching of a few professors who made the Old Testament come alive with relevant meaning. To say that these men were used of God to transform my mind would be a gross understatement, for they did far more. They could draw modern-day parallels from old narratives that made history seem futuristic. They gave me tools so that I could unlock processes of studying the Old Testament to see modern-day meaning.

One such tool was watching for repetition.

The people in antiquity were oral people. Their life and their story were passed down through the generations mainly through the spoken word. And much the same method was used to convey the truths of God's kingdom. People back then knew how to tell a story. And you can bet that people back then also knew how to *listen* when a story was told.

Any time an Old Testament writer repeated a word or a phrase, he was employing repetition to give the listener a sense of intensity. If you go back and read the context surrounding the Shema, you will notice many occasions bridging from chapter 5 into chapter 6 where the writer says something to the effect of "that it may be well with you, and that you may prolong your days in the land." God is working hard to make sure His people don't miss the point: *don't get out of plumb.*

Now think about the Shema.

In terms of parenting getting out of plumb, look at it now through the lens of what happened to the elephant bulls in South Africa. Do you see what happens when things move outside the created order?

When the family breaks down, days on the earth do not *go well*, nor are they *prolonged*. Life, society, and civilization implode when the model God has given us for that life is abandoned.

So again I ask, what happens when both the village *and* the father go missing?

When this happens, boys have no clue what it means to be a man. They have no models for manhood. They have no righteous standard to emulate. And they are left totally abandoned with little hope of discovering what it means to be a man of God.

You and I both know that when young men have no righteous man to look up to, the devil will be sure that a substitute is provided.

OF KNIGHTS AND DAYS PAST

Many years ago, long before Michelle and I had boys of our own, I read a book from Robert Lewis titled *Raising a Modern-Day Knight*. Believing that God would surely give me a son, I felt it was good preparation, and really even good stewardship for the future Hall of Fame golfer and future president of the United States who would be born into my lineage.

See, brother, God is in control of everything, and He knew better than to give me a daughter. I am fully convinced I'd be a terrible dad to a daughter because I would likely be nothing but an emotional, paranoid, skeptical, and downright rude man. I believe she'd be the most beautiful woman to grace her generation, and therefore every male, *every single male* walking the planet, regardless of age or social status, would be nothing but a thief and complete scumbag, not worthy of being in the same room with her for any reason whatsoever.

I even told my wife once, "Hey, just know, if we have a girl, it's not going to be fair to me or to her. I'm just saying, I won't have any objectivity whatsoever. . .on anything."

So God gave me boys.

On a side note: for all you dads out there with daughters who are emotionally well adjusted and still willing to talk to you, you are my heroes.

In Lewis's book, he runs the metaphor of how boys have clean lines of manhood, processes of sorts, that lead them toward being men. He takes us back to a time before the feminization of men, when it wasn't a bad thing to be a man, to think like a man, or to feel like a man.

While it may be weird to promote another book within a book, I absolutely cannot reinforce how desperately you need to read *Raising a Modern-Day Knight* if you have sons. It's not a difficult read, and I am confident you'll not regret reading it.

I first read this book in 1997, the year it was published. When I started down the road of putting my thoughts together for a book of my own, which I was ever-so-creatively listing in my files as "the dad book" because I didn't know what to call it yet, I repurchased Lewis's book and went through it again.

Two decades had passed since I first read it, and I was amazed at how much of it had stuck with me. I was, however, shaken a bit by how Lewis's thoughts and observations were both a clarion call of prediction then and a reason for heartbreak today. I was once again confronted with the brutal reality of how far our culture has declined; I already knew it, for it's easy to see. Yet when I read some of Lewis's insights, I saw it all the more clearly.

MEETING ROBERT LEWIS—SORT OF

Robert and I talked for about an hour on the phone many years ago. As I recall, it would have been around 2005. The backstories of our lives hold a few small similarities.

We were both pastors. We were both authors. We both had intense passion to lead men toward the kingdom of God, evidenced in our personal and professional lives. And we were both men whom God had called out of pastoring a church to move into the world of men's ministry. Robert had already made the transition, and I was really debating it, though my church didn't know it at the time.

Knowing that Robert had just launched out on his own, and that I was considering doing the same, I called his office. I figured that since he no longer had a staff, I had a much better shot at getting him on the phone.

It worked. Just one day later, after leaving a voice mail, we were talking on the phone. I still remember that phone call.

We spoke for almost an hour, unpacking our hearts to one another about men's issues related to God's kingdom and how churches were seemingly neglecting the agent God called to be the leader of the family: the man.

A MANHOOD LANGUAGE

Lewis makes a striking observation about the progression toward manhood: "Sons need fathers in their lives—dads who will love them, teach them, and discipline them. But clearly, sons also need a masculine vision. They need a *manhood language*."[3]

Lewis made that statement in 1997.

Just yesterday I sat in the office of a mom who is raising a teenage daughter. I saw her shaking her head in complete bewilderment. She was showing me an Instagram post where a

Hollywood celebrity was being heralded as a hero by people all over the world because this celebrity used the "proper" transgender pronoun—*they*—to refer to a teenager instead of *him* or *her*.

To be clear, the teenager in the post doesn't make any reference to being transgender. No, the celebrity seems to have merely been working hard to be politically correct. That's how I interpreted it.

To demonstrate, I'll change the names so as not to get sued, and you'll have no idea who I'm referring to. This person to whom the celebrity was referring had a name that could be that of either a boy or a girl. I'll randomly pick the name Taylor.

Again, for the sake of clarity, in this social media post, I have no idea if "Taylor" was a boy or a girl. The picture made it hard to tell. Let's say hypothetically, for the sake of argument, that Taylor is a teenage girl.

The social media post *should* have read—and by "should have" I'm referring not to anything moral but purely lexical—something akin to, "I'm so proud of Taylor. She is doing great in life."

No harm. No foul.

Oh, wait. I forgot. I apologize. It's 2017.

Huge harm. Huge foul. Very foul indeed.

And mean.

Not just mean: hateful. And uneducated.

Call *Good Morning America*, and call them now! We have a hate monger looming out there in society.

To refer to someone like that is so, so, so barbaric. Completely insensitive. And it must be stopped. Today. Censor that man today. Yes, I must be stripped of my career too, because I am an endangerment to society at large. Literally, I'm putting lives at stake.

Never mind that there's this thing called the First Amendment. Never mind that common sense isn't so common anymore. Forget all of that.

Who am I to label someone and judge them and be so cruel? How could I be so anti-intellectual as to refer to a woman as— wait for it—a female?

The post actually read something like—and I'm loosely quoting from memory—"I'm so happy for Taylor. They are doing great in life."

This celebrity was heralded and applauded by thousands upon thousands as being someone who is relevant and genuinely loving due to the use of the appropriate pronoun *they*, because it doesn't judge Taylor or put boundaries on Taylor's life.

Here we are, my friends. Here we are. We are now in a culture that is making every attempt to disregard anatomy and reinvent language.

Has anyone done the math on this? Has anyone forecasted where this is going?

If this anti-intellectual circus continues, we won't even be able to speak to one another in a few years.

I am serious.

If we keep this up, words will have to be outlawed.

You think I'm being dramatic?

The first time I ever heard the term *politically correct* I was driving down the road listening to talk radio. I'd put that memory somewhere around the year 2000 or 2001. I remember thinking, *There is no way an educated society, no matter how liberal or conservative, will ever be so moronic as to adopt anything this intellectually stupid and condescending as being politically correct.*

Well?

Here we are.

People, *good people,* are losing their careers today because they stepped on politically correct land mines. Liberal people, conservative people, men, and women, are losing their jobs over things like a Tweet that somehow got mismanaged or misrepresented. *Poof!* They said something that wasn't politically correct enough, and their jobs are gone.

If this keeps up, society at large will be forced to abandon words. Words, all of them, every single word in any language, will become so mean and so risky—yes, risky—that we must avoid the use of them. By using words, we place people at risk of such irreversible psychological trauma that their mental health is at stake. Thus words must be banned.

That's where this is going.

Ours is a confused world where truth has given way to completely mindless worldviews.

Lewis never could have known how prophetic his simple idea

of "language" would become just twenty years later. Language, as it turns out, is at center stage today. We are, literally, living in a culture that is attempting to redefine the very words we use to distinguish something as simple as male and female human beings.

And there is no way that any of us who follow Jesus could have seen the erosion, and the devastation from that erosion, of the culture in which our boys and girls are being raised today.

CULTURE TODAY

I do feel Lewis to be a prophet.

He, among others, saw it coming. He didn't know what it would look like or how far gone we would be. However, a man possessing any basic intelligence at all can see in Lewis's writing that there is impending danger on the horizon for boys on the journey toward manhood.

Consider Lewis's ability to see it unfold:

> Every son needs a Code Of Conduct. This "weapon of the spirit" becomes even more imperative when you consider the immoral character of modern society. Gone are the days when infractions like talking out of turn, or chewing gum, or running in the halls were con-sidered major problems. Today the challenges

require on-site police officers, metal detectors, and grief counselors.[4]

Again, Lewis wrote these words in 1997. How chilling they are in hindsight, with the Columbine massacre but a couple years away, taking place on April 20, 1999. And Columbine being just a precursor to evils seen at Sandy Hook on December 14, 2012.

Culture has broken down and left boys and girls without righteous role models in the form of real men who love God and stand for His pathways that build a society from the home up.

When men, *righteous* men, are absent from the scene, you'll see the Pilanesberg elephant catastrophe take on human form.

Neither you nor I need to execute a comprehensive sociological experiment to come to the conclusion that the family as we know it has been in jeopardy for a long, long time. Today's culture is overflowing with broken, fatherless homes.

The home matters to God. In fact, God created the family before He created the church. He started creation with the family, not the church.

The family matters to God. And when you remove the idea of a God-defined family from society, what happens next? All of the powers of hell break loose on this world. The part in all of this that I struggle with the most goes far deeper, however.

The Shema took into account that God's people were of the same mind and of the same heart. They lived and breathed and worked and played in community with one another. Life was shared holistically. That doesn't appear to be happening as much anymore.

INCUBATORS

The Shema took into account that families were intact. At least that's how society worked back then; and in reality, that's how society worked up until we began to see divorce on demand after 1960. The family, with all of its problems, stayed together then. Or, at least it's fair to say, the family stayed together at a much higher rate than that it does now.

The idea of family, and family values, has all but disappeared. Families seem to exist now as incubators for a child's dreams to come true.

I've coached my sons' baseball and football teams every year they've been in sports. I absolutely love it. And through coaching, I've been able to see society's values, and what families value, playing out before my very eyes.

Dads all around me work tirelessly to provide $200 DeMarini bats, so that a son may have dreams fulfilled and psyche healed, through things like travel baseball or maybe the

> THE IDEA OF FAMILY, AND FAMILY VALUES, HAS ALL BUT DISAPPEARED. FAMILIES SEEM TO EXIST NOW AS INCUBATORS FOR A CHILD'S DREAMS TO COME TRUE

hope of a college scholarship.

Never mind that the kid cannot hit a baseball to save his life. Perhaps if the dad would actually spend time in the yard teaching the boy how to catch a baseball, something magical would happen—so much more than a $200 bat and a $100 glove can provide.

Dream incubators—that is what we have become as parents in the modern era.

Moms are now not so much mamas, the women who are the queens of the home, but something more akin to that of professional taxi drivers with nice vehicles. Instead of driving a yellow car, they carry out their Uber-like pursuits in minivans and SUVs complete with Wi-Fi, so that their teenage daughters won't miss anything their friends are doing on Snapchat. God forbid that they actually talk face-to-face.

So Mom and Dad live, and have as their mission in life, to provide, or should I say fund, the magic incubator that magically turns out well-adjusted young adults.

MY CULTURE THEN

Author William Kilpatrick wrote in *Why Johnny Can't Tell Right from Wrong*, "Parents cannot, as they once did, rely on the culture to reinforce home values. In fact, they can expect that many of the cultural forces influencing their children will be actively undermining those values."[5]

Kilpatrick penned those words in 1992.

Staggering, isn't it?

Today *family* can mean just about anything. Very little of it has anything to do with what we see in concepts like the Shema. And that means that the role of being a Christlike dad is harder than it has ever been.

It means that while God intended the community to help us raise our boys, the community has imploded in many ways because we abandoned His model for life. God didn't abandon the model. We did.

The cold, hard truth is that being a dad, and being a dad resolved to follow the Lord God, is perhaps more critical, and more lonely, than it has ever been before in history.

No matter how hard it may be, or how hard it may get, you and I cannot collapse in the journey. We as fathers cannot collapse under the grind. Our children deserve so much more than passivity.

5

WHAT MY SONS DESERVE FROM ME

I hate entitlement. I'm using the word *hate* here. And I mean to use it.

I hate entitlement because it's an entitlement mentality that is killing America. I take every chance I get to remind my sons that there is no such thing as a free lunch. Someone somewhere had to pay for the free lunch, and I want them to realize that. They need to know that this world does not owe them anything. They are not entitled to a job. Or a house. Or amenities. Or end-of-the-year bonuses.

Nevertheless, I do believe my sons are deserving of certain things from me.

MY SONS DESERVE A DAD WHO LIVES OUT BIBLICAL MANHOOD

It's impossible to be a perfect dad. But that's no excuse for not striving to live out biblical manhood. I must be fully committed to the heart of God, and that most certainly governs not just how

I live but the way I raise my sons.

I can seek to be their best friend and have them like me. I can seek to be the cool dad on every front. In doing that, however, I may miss the target completely in terms of honoring God with the way I parent.

Jesus said quite a bit about priority and perspective. While I realize He wasn't talking at all about parenting, He was speaking about the very nature of discipleship in Mark 8:36 when He said, "For what does it profit a man to gain the whole world, and forfeit his soul?"

Is parenting about discipleship?

Only to the extent that oxygen is necessary for breathing.

If I seek to be my sons' BFF, I may gain their admiration yet forfeit their souls to the highest bidder. That's right, my sons' souls are my responsibility—at least in the early years.

I can in no way secure their eternal destiny, but God has placed them under my care. They are under my watch. Like a night watchman, I am standing on the wall, well armed physically and spiritually, always at the ready.

I am commissioned by God to be their soul coach.

Fathers, do not provoke your children to anger,
but bring them up in the discipline and instruction
of the Lord.
EPHESIANS 6:4

That is God's commission to me, which therefore means I must take my own walk with God extremely seriously. My boys must see me walking the path of Christ, fully committed without compromise to the nature and heart of God.

MY SONS DESERVE A DAD WHO IS INTENTIONAL ABOUT RAISING THEM WITH CONVICTIONS THAT HOLD UP UNDER PRESSURE

The reason I rail against pop culture so openly and aggressively is simply because nothing in pop culture is eternal. Nothing in pop culture lasts, nor is it designed to do so.

I grew up in the 1970s and '80s. My parents wore platform shoes and bell bottoms. My dad had an afro that would make Dr. J green with envy—and it was all hip.

And it is now all in the past.

In the '80s, I attended my first prom looking like Don Johnson on *Miami Vice*. White suit, mango-colored V-neck T-shirt, complete with leather loafers with no socks—and it was all hip.

And it is now all in the past.

Pop culture icons today tell us all what they told us then: here's what cool *looks like*. As adults, however, we all know that *cool* is a moving target.

Pop culture worships at the altar of materialism, envy, and consumerism, whose god, as Paul said in Philippians 3:18–20, is its "belly" or "appetite."

*For many walk, of whom I often told you, and now
tell you even weeping, that they are enemies of the
cross of Christ, whose end is destruction, whose god is
their appetite, and whose glory is in their shame, who
set their minds on earthly things. For our citizenship
is in heaven, from which also we eagerly wait for a
Savior, the Lord Jesus Christ.*

It's not that pop culture is all wrong all the time. Each era and each season of life has a ton of fun about it. Look, I was cool in that Don Johnson wardrobe. We all know it. I'm not sure my date to the dance knew it, but I knew it.

It's not that pop culture has it all wrong; it's just that pop culture isn't eternal.

So let's use fashion to talk about being a dad.

When I was in college, I was a clotheshorse. The label inside the collar of my shirt mattered, and buddy, I was going to have the best clothes and look sharp no matter what.

Then I grew up.

I was telling a millennial friend of mine not long ago, "You'll know you've turned a corner when you honestly just don't care about clothes anymore and you are completely unwilling to pay $40 for a pair of jeans."

I gave up on fashion because fashion is a moving target. As a man who has been hunting since the age of five, I can promise you that a moving target is the hardest target to hit.

There is something deeper here beyond the jabs I'm making about clothes. I am not willing to let pop culture tell me what I should value.

And the reason I'm not willing is because modern culture doesn't value the kingdom of God. Back to Paul's premise: they have *set their minds on earthly things.*

If my sons want to place a value on clothing, so be it. I don't really care. What I do care about is that they never see their worth measured by what they can purchase. My sons deserve more, but I must teach them what *more* is, and I must teach them how more is *defined*, in light of the eternal. And this is why a dad must have concrete convictions about biblical manhood. Convictions matter.

We have a name for convictions in Christendom: theology. And theology matters. I cringe every time I hear a preacher say something akin to, "Now I'm not going to give you some big theological sermon today."

Look man, theology matters. Theology is the ball game, my brother. Why? Because what you believe drives how you act.

My sons need—no, my sons *deserve*—a dad who teaches them not about being hip, but about timeless truths relative to the nature and character of God as played out in everyday, mundane life.

WHAT YOU BELIEVE DRIVES HOW YOU ACT

As a dad, I must see my son's spiritual growth as something unpacked for the next sixty years, not the next sixty months. And for that to happen, I must be committed to who he will become, not just how he'll be accepted by his peers in the tenth grade.

He deserves a dad who will model those convictions in his own life so that his son doesn't see him as a man tall on words and short on action.

MY SON DESERVES A DAD WITH A PLAN

I love farmers.

No kidding, I really love farmers. They are becoming my heroes.

I love how they move slowly. I love how they are just straight-up, wise dudes.

My family owns a little piece of land on the Mississippi Delta. So I took a good friend of mine and our boys down to Mississippi one time for a duck hunt. I felt like we probably had enough ammo for the occasion, but we decided to go buy some more shotgun shells because we didn't want our boys to run out of ammunition on what we hoped would be an epic duck hunt the next morning.

My friend and I left the boys at the house while we drove into town. My songwriting buddy and I had joined up with my friend James, a local man born and raised on the Delta. We all walked into the small store, with James in the lead. As the doors to the small establishment swung open, we could smell the live bait—crickets, minnows—and country life.

I don't think the store owner even turned around. He must have winded James somehow, for he knew exactly who had entered the establishment.

He just said, "Hey, James," and continued to cut a lady's hair as she sat in the barber's chair.

Yes, a barber's chair.

The barber's chair is right next to the live minnow tank. And the live minnow tank is right next to the shelves that hold the shotgun shells.

My famous country songwriter buddy leaned into my ear and said, "Good Lord, bro, you cannot make this place up. Like seriously, this is legit. I want to move here, and I'm not kidding."

That's what I love about the Delta.

You can enter a tiny sporting goods store, pick up a box of shotgun shells, get some live minnows, and get a haircut too.

The fabric of life is real on the Delta. And so is community.

The Farm Supply

Down near our land there is a farm supply store as well. I hesitate to call it a store, but I don't really know what else to call it.

It's a church, sort of. It's kind of a coffee shop. It's an academic institution on some levels. And you can buy poly pipe and Gramoxone there too. And if you want to fill up your tractor with diesel, there's a stand-alone pump behind the store.

Look man, it's everything you imagine it to be. In fact, it's *the* place to be—especially between 7 and 9 a.m. every day of the week (except Sunday). At that time on any given morning, a group of farmers will be sitting in rocking chairs, drinking coffee, and talking about commodity prices, wars, and weather. They'll only pause in their long and intense discussions about weather to talk about why truck manufacturers are embarrassing themselves with the prices they're charging for pickup trucks these days.

The farm supply store cronies are theologically confounded by cultural unicorns such as flat-bill ball caps. Yet you can be sure they will give oral consideration, at length, to the flat-bill cap and discuss it with organic, surprising clarity.

And the flat bill will inevitably lead to discussions as to how they got their own first baseball caps, which will lead to a story on Brooks Robinson and how Brooks was the cousin of a guy they knew back in grade school, which will lead them to talk about how that guy—you know, the cousin of Brooks Robinson—loved to fight, but you had to watch him because he'd pull a knife on you if he was losing the confrontation.

You don't really need television if you have access to the farm supply. All the comedy, politics, and business life you ever want to encounter can be yours to experience right there in those rocking chairs.

Noticers

Farmers are what I would call *noticers*. They notice things. Instead of seeing a crow in the sky, they notice how a crow flies as opposed to how a hawk does it.

They know things too, from all their noticing. Like how a north wind dries out dirt faster than a south wind does, because a south wind holds far more humidity within it. It's these kinds of things that get lost in an iced latte world.

I mentioned my buddy James, the local boy. Not long ago I was down on the Delta with James and my friend Cal, two men who hold places in my heart too dear to put into words. Cal and James grew up about six miles from each other.

And though they had absolutely no reason to do so—no reason whatsoever—they let me into their lives. I tread there with holy paces, for they did not have to let me in. Cal and James have taught me more about what Jesus said about loving thy neighbor as thyself than any book I've ever read on the subject—by far.

Cal is a farmer by choice. He's a good and competent farmer too. Actually, Cal is good at a lot of things. He's a poet. A musician, sort of. He can fix a tractor, and if you've ever seen a tractor up close, that's no small statement. He's a bird-dog romantic. And he holds a master's degree in journalism. He's a Mississippi country boy who married a city girl from New Mexico. Now go and ponder that!

While I have never met Ernest Hemingway, I'd admit that Hemingway is my idea of the quintessential man of epic ruggedness on many levels. Cal is perhaps the closest thing to Ernest Hemingway I've ever met, minus suicidal thoughts and the heavy drinking for which Hemingway was so well known.

I needed to plant corn just to flood it and leave it standing. Flooded corn is the gold standard by which a man may attract many ducks to his hole. The problem is, I am not a farmer. I've planted things before, and I only had to do that once to realize that a person cannot stick seed in the dirt, pray over it, and expect a crop. Having been around farmers all my life, and especially more so in the last ten years, I've been known to say many times, "The next time you eat green beans, just realize that you have absolutely, positively no clue about what it took to get that bean to your fork." And so when it came to planting corn, I wanted to ask Cal a question.

I'm an unashamed, unapologetic extrovert, and still it took me almost three weeks to muster up the courage to take my request to Cal. I wanted to know if he'd *oversee* me in the process of corn planting.

His reply was staggering. I kid you not, the single sentence alone could be the topic of a book. My question went something like this: "Cal, I need to plant corn, but not just any kind of corn. I need corn that will actually come out of the ground and have ears on it. The problem is, Cal, you and I both know full well that I don't know how to plant corn—I mean real corn that works like corn is supposed to, you know? I don't know how to work a planter implement, and I don't know the first thing about proper fertilizer application rates or even how to ask for it at the farm supply. So is there any way you could help me?"

I actually thought about trying to shed a tear when making

the sales pitch. I really did. Not the kind of saline that rolls down your cheek heavy, for I figured he'd surely be keen to the ruse were I to go with heavy saline. I was contemplating something more like a quarter tear, like what you see in a man's eye as he's just about 17 percent choked up. I'd have done it too if I was any good at method acting.

Upon hearing the question, Cal simply said, "Well, Jason, sure I will. I just assumed that came with the friendship."

"I just assumed that came with the friendship."

I'm telling you, there's a book in there somewhere. A big, fat theological book about Jesus' idea of *neighbor*, but that's for another time.

Sowing

The day came when we finally synchronized our schedules, and we went out to plant corn. I cannot, with the support of any lexicon, describe how excited I was when the sun came up that morning.

I do believe I know what woke me so early that morning. I think it had to do with the possibility that I might now be *included*. No longer would I be like the lawman who knew something of the law but had never arrested a real criminal. I believed that from this day forward I could drink coffee at the farm supply and talk about farming. Real. American. Farming.

I knew that I was just one day's matriculation from being able to talk about Roundup Ready Soybeans and know that they are green in the bag, coated with this purplish green stuff, instead of looking like a blond seed that some novice might expect.

I envisioned being able to talk about topics like herbicide, and know when it is to be used for ultimate effect. In my mind, I'd made the papal transition necessary to join the rocking chair conversations.

With the day of planting now a reality, I was struck by many things about the planting process. Yet nothing, and I mean *nothing*, struck me as much as Cal's deliberation. His calculating and discussing and estimating seemingly went on for hours.

He was like a pitcher who takes the mound, only to stare down the hitter for an excruciating length of time because he knows the batter is no match for him, nor is the batter worthy to say he faced a pitcher of his caliber.

And thus the pitcher crushes the batter's soul with anticipation as his weapon. The man on the mound knows his weapon is not the ball but the *anticipation* that a pitch is coming, so that by the time the pitch gets there, the batter's mind is so overcome with emotion that he cannot bear to hit it.

We finally got the planter hitched to the tractor, and I just knew that we were about to execute the plan. We drove down the dusty gravel road and made a move south on the turn row.

It would only be seconds now.

I drove the truck down to the lower area of the farm in case we needed it for anything. In my rearview mirror, I was watching Cal's hand. He'd be reaching for the hydraulics any moment.

Anticipation. . . Continued

We got to the field surrounding my duck hole, and what did Cal do but get off the tractor. He got off the tractor. Like a pitcher who just can't bring himself to close the deal, he backed off at the very moment of truth.

I got out of my truck and walked right at him, all of my love for the man hidden under a bushel basket of frustration. Still, I remained silent.

Cal asked, "You have a tape measure?"

Walking back toward my truck, I said, "Cal, what in the world could you possibly need a tape measure for, man? I'm not Bob Vila, and this ain't carpentry. This is the world of Farmall and DEKALB seeds."

Cal just looked at me. Right through me he looked, as if to say, "Just shut up and go get me a tape measure."

I did have a tape measure on hand.

And I knew I did. It was in the bed of my truck, inside the huge toolbox that I'd brought for the day of planting.

If there was one thing I had learned, from being around and hunting with and being loved on by such giants as commercial farmer Kirk Whitmore, who is a true Arkansas legend in my mind, was that a man had better be ready at any given moment to fix any given thing when on a farm.

And so I had my tools on hand. At least I knew enough to bring them.

I got the tape measure and was nearly bursting with

questions about why we needed it. I figured I was soon to find out, so I kept my mouth shut—an Olympic feat in and of itself.

Cal just said, "Stand here and hold it."

It wasn't even a request. It was a command. And a condescending edict at that, issued forth to a man of my education and global travel experience. I have been paid well for decades to speak at conferences to thousands upon thousands of weary souls needing my exegetical depth. Yet here I was soaked in the heat of the Mississippi sun where my journey had come full circle to "Stand here and hold it."

Standing in a field full of dirt with the looming potential of a cottonmouth encounter at any given second, I had been reduced to knowing my place in the agricultural community.

I was a doctoral degree-owning holder of the tape measure.

Cal proceeded to measure out 14 feet 5 inches. At the zero mark, he dragged his boot and made a line across the Delta dirt, the very dirt that I'd just disked the day before. He walked to the 14-feet-5-inch mark and dragged another line.

He got back on the tractor, dropped the planter, and made a complete pass through that zone of 14 feet 5 inches.

He hopped off the tractor.

He then explained to me that using that measurement you can pretty well know your seed population per acre. The old planter we were using was on 36-inch centers, which is what our CASE 800 was set to, and it would drop seed accordingly.

And 14 feet 5 inches was the equivalent of an acre for seed population.

See, that's the kind of eternal wisdom you'll never—and I mean *never*—obtain, nor have access to, at Starbucks.

They sell coffee too, but not the kind of coffee like the farm supply gives away for free. Instead of a scone, your free farm supply coffee comes complete with why you need to know about 36-inch centers and tape measures.

And Then It Was Over

Cal hopped back on the tractor, dropped that CASE 800 planter with authority, and buddy, he took off. My tillable acreage surrounding the duck hole is right at four acres, and he was done in about fourteen minutes.

Among many other things, this is what I learned that day: once you plant that seed, it's over. There's no getting that stuff out of the ground. So you'd better be real sure about what you're doing.

If you're not sure, you're going to cry rivers of tears. And they won't be method-acting tears either, like those tears I was fully prepared to manufacture to get Cal to perform his agricultural magic. No, they'll be real tears, because your wallet, and thus your ability to feed your family, is going to suffer from your lack of planning and preparation.

What I learned that day was that the hard work—the really, really hard work, the dirty work full of grime and grit and thought,

the work that makes the most difference—is done in the preparation and planting process.

To plant and plant well, with the kind of corn that will actually come out of the ground, means that you need a plan.

My sons deserve a dad who has a plan.

You must sow before you reap.

6

SOWING MANHOOD

When my wife and I had our first son, Cole, I was determined that he enter manhood better prepared for it than I was when I took off on my own. I didn't really know how I'd go about it, but I was determined to craft something—*anything*—that would give me some measure of a plan.

Modeling manhood through traditional examples of "watch me" is critical, but modeling isn't enough on its own. We must be sure to speak what we want to see in the lives of our sons. We must say it. We cannot afford to hope that they just "get it" by noticing. Too much is at stake because the marketplace of culture is coming at them without mercy.

Children are now target markets.

Children are demographic sets of data that companies go after ruthlessly. There's no shielding our sons from the freight train of life. That train was moving much slower when we were their age. There are now no restrictions, no honor; nothing is off-limits anymore when it comes to getting access to our sons' future purchasing habits.

I do not want my sons to enter into manhood unprepared. So *I* must sow, before *my sons* can reap.

Make sure you didn't miss that: *I* must sow, before *my sons* can reap.

If I don't lay down the plan, if I am not the chief architect laying out what manhood looks like, then I can rest assured that the world will draft a plan for my sons and install it well within them.

The problem with planning is that I'm not really great at doing it. I far prefer to live in the moment. But as I've gotten older, I've learned that a plan doesn't have to be complex to be effective.

Plans do not have to be complex; they just have to be defined and carried out. Slow down for a second and let that sink in. Plans do not need to be perfect because perfection is an impossible expectation. You cannot have the perfect plan for raising a boy because life is constantly imperfect.

> **PLANS DO NOT HAVE TO BE COMPLEX; THEY JUST HAVE TO BE DEFINED AND CARRIED OUT**

Life moves left when you thought it would move right. Life morphs and throws you curves—like cancer, or job loss, or divorce, or a son who decides later on in life that he wants to experiment with being gay.

You cannot have the perfect plan. And God isn't asking you for perfection. He is asking you to be wise. Look for yourself and you'll see God calling you to wisdom throughout the entire book of Proverbs. And wisdom dictates that you cannot expect your son to know how to navigate manhood if you do not at least have some measure of a plan.

BACK TO KNIGHTHOOD

Perhaps the greatest contribution that Robert Lewis gave future fathers like me in 1997 when he wrote *Raising a Modern-Day Knight* was the idea of what he calls "a clearly designed path."[1]

His idea of progression was monumental for me. For the first time, I could see a model, a plan that I could follow once I had boys of my own. Lewis illustrated the path to becoming a knight: a boy started as a page, worked toward becoming a squire, and then was eligible for the role of knight. I carried this mental image with me for a long time. I knew then that when God gave me sons of my own, I needed to make sure that I had laid out a path of some kind. And so I did.

ELIMINATING EXCUSES

I have a concealed weapon carry permit.

When I went from just owning a gun to carrying a gun, I experienced a major shift in mentality. I've still not mastered it. My friend Ken, who owns and operates a small defense training company, said it best one day as we were discussing carrying a gun on your person: "It's really a lifestyle. You have to force yourself to realize that you owe it to yourself, and your family, to avoid being a victim. You have the right not to be a victim. And so you must fully commit to it."

Ken is right.

I struggled at first to find the right gun. I tried a standard size .40 caliber but found myself leaving it in the truck more than having it on my person. It was bulky. Eventually I traded that gun for a smaller gun, often referred to as a subcompact. And that gun worked for a while, but I began to notice that it wasn't completely working for me. So I made a trip to the gun store. The guys in there know me well, and I trust their judgment, especially Mike's, one of the owners. He's a gentle guy and always full of insight.

I began to explain my issues about carrying to Mike—not feeling like the gun fit my body and being uncomfortable with the position of where I was carrying it on my waist, which were really just complaints about the whole process.

Mike then said, "The real problem is that many people just simply pick the wrong gun. They pick a big gun or a full-size gun when they first buy a gun for the purpose of carrying." That is exactly what I'd done.

Mike made the truth even clearer by saying, "You must eliminate excuses not to carry. That's the bigger problem. For instance, you'll talk yourself out of carrying to the grocery store because at the moment you have shorts on with no belt—but the truth is—you might need your gun at any given moment. It's no safer to be without a gun on a quick errand than it is, let's say, when you know you're about to go downtown to a big city where crime is more likely. Crime is always a possibility. And so the .380 in your pocket is better than your .40 at home."

Man, did that phrase go deep with me, *"The .380 in your pocket is better than your .40 at home."* It was Mike's way of saying that enacting a simple plan of being prepared is better—way, way better—than a strong and perfect plan sitting in your closet.

ON MAKING FIRST PLANS

I never wrote down my first plans for raising boys. So let that bring you peace! I knew their formative years mattered, so I focused on foundational things. However, 98 percent of dads have no real plan whatsoever for raising boys. Their worldview, even if it is biblical, lives in their heads, but they have no strategy to work.

Like my gun store owner friend Mike said, "The .380 in your pocket is better than your .40 at home." Any plan in action is better than no plan at all.

BE CAREFUL THAT YOU DON'T STEAL

I'm going to share with you some of the foundational principles I've used in preparing my sons on their journey toward manhood. Yet I hesitate to do so because I know men. I know me too. Both you and I are prone to take someone else's idea and say, "Hey, I'll just do that too since it worked for him."

Do not steal my ideas about raising boys. Look, I don't have property rights to parenting philosophies, so of course you could use my ideas. The issue at hand, however, is that you need to dig your manhood models out of your own heart and soul based on what your son needs from you. Seriously. Nobody knows your son like you do. Nobody knows how he moves through life better than you do.

Therefore I cannot possibly know if what works for me will actually work for you. I'm hesitant to show what I've been doing because too many men will just copy my plan and check it off their lists without wrestling with the formulation of their own plan—and that's what matters, that you wrestle with it. Your plan needs to be organic with you, based on who your son is and what he is facing.

Nonetheless, in the pages that follow, I'll share with you what I've done and what I am doing. Take my plan, use it, but be sure to customize it.

Let's move on to the practical application of sowing.

#1

POUR A FOUNDATION OF APPROVAL

You've probably heard it said a hundred times that the foundation is the most important part of the home. It seems I've heard that all of my life too. However, it dawned on me one day that I'd never had anyone explain it to me. I knew that the foundation was the most critical part, but I didn't know why. I just assumed everyone was right when they said it.

And so I asked, "Why?"

Einstein said, "If you can't explain it to a six-year-old, you don't understand it yourself."[2] Simple doesn't mean simplistic, and I wanted a simple explanation of a foundation. I knew I had the perfect source to explain it to me.

I have a friend who is a civil engineer with a master's degree from a prestigious institution. He has built structures all over America. So I called him one day with my query. Though the conversation was many years ago, I remember it well—perhaps because he made it so simple!

Here's how he explained the importance of a good foundation to me.

> It basically comes down to gravity. Gravity always wins. You can never beat gravity, but you can slow down the effect of gravity. So think of it this way: if your foundation is weak, gravity will pull on it and cause major problems early in the life of the structure. If your foundation is well built, then it will delay the costs of repair for years and maybe even decades.
>
> You're going to have to fix the building. There's no getting around that. The question comes down to when do you want to fix the building: in year

five or in year fifty?

From the very beginning, I wanted to pour a foundation that was solid in each of my sons, and I felt that making sure they had my approval was a great place to begin.

Even though they were small in stature and just beginning life, I wanted each of my sons to hear and to feel my approval of them: *"I'm for you. I'm on your side. I'm with you. I'm in favor of you."* You get the point.

From the outset, I wanted each of my sons to know that he met and exceeded any expectation I ever had. He was my son, and I was proud of him.

The apostle Peter wrote, "Above all, keep fervent in your love for one another, because love covers a multitude of sins" (1 Peter 4:8). Peter, this headstrong leader, came back to the foundation of what Jesus said was most important: loving God and loving your neighbor as yourself (Matthew 22:36–40). Peter obviously remembered that love is the foundation of a godly life. He reminded Christ followers that no matter how much they may revile the pagan ways of the culture they live in, they must never forget that love must, *love has to*, undergird all they do.

Love does truly cover a multitude of sins.

Love also covers a multitude of mistakes! From the beginning, I knew I'd make mistakes as a dad. I knew that I would, because a man is going to get things wrong time and again. However, I also knew this: if my sons knew that through it all I was for them, that I loved them, and that I approved of them, they would remember my approval forever. So approval had to be at the foundation of my plan.

Love that is real is love that is spoken.

Oh, my friend, how I hope you never, ever forget that.

You and I both know that love can be spoken but not be real. However, you cannot love from the heart and keep it silent.

And I do believe I can prove it.

> **LOVE THAT IS REAL IS LOVE THAT IS SPOKEN**

BAPTISMS AND LOVE SPOKEN

A strange and seemingly "off the beaten path" thing happened the very moment Jesus was baptized.

A man's baptism is the day of days. I think that's true because men are so visual by nature. The day I went under the water and came back up, I had a feeling of separation from my sin. I knew that Christ had ransomed me the day I repented, but the visual effect of baptism made my being set apart seem even more real.

We call God the "Father." He is the ultimate father. Slow down your mind a bit and think that through. God is a father. A dad.

And His Son was having His own day of days. Matthew gives the account this way:

Then Jesus arrived from Galilee at the Jordan coming to John, to be baptized by him. But John tried to prevent Him, saying, "I have need to be baptized by You, and do You come to me?"

But Jesus answering said to him, "Permit it at this time; for in this way it is fitting for us to fulfill all righteousness." Then he permitted Him.

After being baptized, Jesus came up immediately from the water; and behold, the heavens were opened, and he saw the Spirit of God descending as a dove and lighting on Him, and behold, a voice out of the heavens said, "This is My beloved Son, in whom I am well-pleased."

MATTHEW 3:13–17

WHY DID GOD SAY THAT?

Why did God speak love over His Son? He didn't have to do it—but He did.

No words in scripture are wasted. So the fact that God spoke for all the crowd to hear was and is critical to our understanding of His nature as a father.

God's Son was human.

I am not sure that most Christians really believe that though. I'm serious. Most Christians have a hard time grasping that Jesus was fully man—that is, fully God and yet fully man. Sure,

Christians will tell you they believe it, but how most Christians actually *talk* about Jesus as a human being is a different story altogether. We get the "fully God" part down. That sits well with us in our minds. Miracles came forth from Jesus' words. He could walk on water.

The "fully man" concept? Not so much.

Listen to how Christians talk about Jesus, and you'll hear in their words this perception that Jesus was immune from life. His temptation wasn't really as difficult, for He was Jesus. Like Superman, only real.

That's heresy. Jesus was fully human.

And that meant He felt pain when the soldiers whipped His back. He felt real temptation—real temptation—when a woman swung her hips and walked a certain way past the carpenter's shop. And when a customer said cruel things about His carpentry products, He felt the sting.

Jesus was human. And Jesus was a son. And every son needs the love of a dad to be spoken over him.

Listen to what God the Father said at Jesus' baptism: "This is My beloved Son. . . ."

This was a proud Dad talking. *"That's my Boy right there! Look at Him. He's letting all the world know about His faith."*

Yes, Jesus was most likely about age thirty by then, but it didn't change the fact that a proud Father spoke His love and pleasure over His Son for the whole world to hear.

THE GREAT LIE ABOUT LOVE SPOKEN

I cringe with disgust every time I hear a man say something akin to, "My family knows I love them. I don't have to say it. It's just not my way."

The first thought in my mind is, *Who are you trying to convince, me or you?* It's a lie, and that man is lying to himself because he assumes his family knows of his love for them.

Guess what? They *don't* know!

Do you know how I know that?

In a word: *funerals*.

I've spoken at a lot of funerals, and all too often I hear from the kids of that kind of dad, the one who never spoke love yet just *knew* that his kids knew he loved them. Now in their forties, they say things like, "Daddy never did tell us he loved us, but I believe that he did."

Let me clarify what they are really trying to say in that moment when the casket is about seventeen feet behind their left shoulder and people are standing around making small talk about this man whose body is now cold and lifeless. They are really trying to say, "I think my dad loved me. I mean, I hope he did, but I can't really be sure about it because he never said he did. He was a provider, and I suppose that's love."

> **PROVIDING FOR YOUR FAMILY ISN'T THE SAME THING AS LOVING THEM**

Providing for your family isn't the same thing as loving them.

Far too many men think that love is provision. Love, however, is not provision. Providing for your family is a form of responsibility. You owe it to your family to provide for them. Love is both an emotion and a promise. And those two go hand in hand. So providing for your family is a by-product of love manifested in things like a home and 401(k). Real love, however, is spoken, just as God the Father spoke love over His Son.

EVERY SINGLE DAY

As a boy, I heard my dad tell me every day, "I love you." He'd say it as I was going to bed. Or it might show up in all sorts of other contexts. Mama said it every day too.

I had my dad's approval. He spoke it over me. Whether I tanked and shot 82 in a golf tournament, or whether I brought home the champion's trophy, his love was constant. And spoken. I knew I didn't have to earn his approval. It was foundational to everything I felt and knew: I had his favor.

I am determined to do the same for my boys.

#2
DISCIPLINE: LOVE THROUGH ACCOUNTABILITY

My daddy spanked me. More than once.

Let me be real clear here: my daddy never beat me or mistreated me. It's a shame that in today's world we have to provide such disclaimers. They are a new reality of this absurd, emotionally fragile world in which we now live.

Spanking and abuse are completely different concepts. Spanking is *not* abuse. Abuse is abuse.

Look, I know that some of you reading this book were abused by your fathers. I've walked with many men who felt the pain of literal beatings from their fathers. That's awful. And it's tragic. However, spanking is in no way related to beating.

IF YOU DO IT RIGHT YOU WON'T DO IT OFTEN

Here's what I've learned from being in the thick of it raising boys: if you spank them early, you won't have to spank them often.

In all honesty, I don't remember getting a spanking after the age of five or six years old. I didn't need one, man. I knew from the tone of my dad's voice that if I did "that" again, whatever *that* was at the moment, I'd be paying for it.

My daddy was never mean to me, and my daddy was never hard on me, but my daddy spanked me. He was a firm believer that bad decisions and pain always go together!

My dad taught me through spanking that life has boundaries. And if I trespass beyond those boundaries, I'll pay the price. The New Living Translation says, "Those who spare the rod of discipline hate their children. Those who love their children care enough to discipline them" (Proverbs 13:24).

"Care enough." That's what spanking is: caring enough to teach your son that pain does go with bad decisions.

How can my son ever know he's a sinner in need of a Savior if I don't teach him that sin has consequences?

Sin does have painful consequences. Life has boundaries. Step outside those boundaries in life, and life will spank you with harsh, quick reminders.

My sons must understand that now.

PAIN AND BAD DECISIONS

Let me tell you what I've learned about life: if I make a bonehead decision at the age of forty-four, life is going to spank me. And when life spanks me, it's going to hurt worse than any spanking Daddy ever gave me.

It turns out, my dad was a genius! Pain and bad decisions do go together!

I fully understand that every child responds to various forms of discipline differently. You can't spank a child for every little thing. You've lost control of yourself if you've taken that approach.

Cole is the kind of boy I have to tread easily with or he'll be crushed under my displeasure. If I indicate the slightest form of disapproval, he's ruined. Tears flow. Heart breaks. Cole is a people pleaser in many ways, and I'm coaching him out of that, but if I overlook the fact that it's in his DNA, he'll suffer for it.

Nevertheless, there were times when I had to punish Cole with a spanking, because time-outs cannot teach certain truths. Time-outs cannot reinforce the coupling of pain and bad decisions.

Can you imagine someone in 1972 trying to explain the parental concept of time-out to my dad? My goodness! I'd love to have been around to have heard that conversation.

SWIMMING UPSTREAM

I realize that spanking is controversial today. Then again, it seems everything in today's culture is controversial because Americans are so sensitive and emotionally fragile.

James Dobson, in his work *Bringing Up Boys*, said the following about culture shifts. Read it slowly, keeping in mind that it was written in 2001:

> The key is for parents to avoid extremes on either side. Over the course of the past 150 years, parental attitudes have swung radically—from oppressiveness and rigidity at one end of the continuum to permissiveness and wimpiness at the other. . . . By the late fifties and early sixties, parents had become decidedly permissive. What was called the "child-centered" approach tended to undermine authority and create little terrors at home. . . . Still, it is my opinion that parents today are more confused than ever about effective and loving discipline. It has become a lost art, a forgotten skill. . . .

People have become less traditional over time with a shift from emphasizing obedience and parent-centered families to valuing autonomy for children. Parents now expect their children to be self-disciplined.[3]

When I read what Dobson had to say about parents expecting kids to be "self-disciplined," I was stung by the reminder of how many times I've overheard parents at a store, a ballpark, or a church lecturing their kids in the same way one might reason with an adult.

You cannot rationalize or reason with a four-year-old!

Do you know how this form of self-disciplined expectation for kids shows up today? I'll give you one example: counting.

Yes, counting. The whole "I said, 'Come here.' One, two, and if I get to three. . ."

Let's play this out.

MEET TYLER

The situation: your little boy, Tyler, is playing in the street.

Parent: Tyler, come here. Now!

Why the insistent command from you? Why the intensity? What Tyler doesn't know, because Tyler cannot see past the tree line, is that there is a dump truck coming down the road about a quarter mile away.

You can see around the curve because you're about 100 yards away. Tyler can most certainly hear you, but you cannot physically get to him fast enough.

Tyler keeps on playing in the street. Why? Because Tyler knows you're not the boss.

Oh, he heard you just fine, but that's irrelevant to him. You've never really established respect, and you've never backed up your word, and Tyler knows it.

He also knows that you usually back down because you want to be the cool dad at the pool party who every kid thinks is hip. And when you do really get mad, Tyler knows it's just going to mean ten minutes of being docked from the Xbox. No big deal. See, playing in the street is way, way more fun because Tyler knows how to play the game that's about to unfold.

You count to one, and then your voice goes up with intensity as you get to two. Tyler knows this because you and Tyler play the game daily—and he's better at it than you are.

> Parent: Tyler, come here *now! One!* (This is when the counting starts.)

Tyler knows that he doesn't want to be put in time-out, but he also knows you've not counted to two yet, so he's still ignoring you. At two and a half he'll obey. He doesn't like time-out. It cramps his style. You can be sure, however, that he'll obey on his terms, not on your terms. He's determined to remain in control.

> Parent: Tyler, run to me now! *Two!* (It always helps if you scream it.)

And now Tyler is dead. His lifeless body is lying in the road.

The dump truck driver is trying to stop, and smoke is everywhere from his brakes locking up. He just couldn't stop on time because he was moving at 48 mph and never saw Tyler until he rounded the curve.

Yes, Tyler is dead.

You can stop counting now.

SERIOUSLY?

You might be thinking, *Wow, that's quite an exaggerated piece of drama you played out right there, Jason.*

Is it? Are you sure about that?

I don't think it's drama at all actually.

OBEDIENCE IS URGENT

In fact, I know it's not drama. Obedience is critical, and there are times when obedience is critical to survival.

Obedience is urgent, but few parents see the outcome as urgent. Few parents see obedience in terms of the long game. They rarely think about what obedience now will mean ten years from now; but obedience is taught today, not ten years from now.

Don't expect your son to respect you when he is sixteen or to live with an understanding that life outside the boundaries will get him hurt if you don't see the urgency in obedience now when he's six.

The one thing I never—and I mean *never*—did when Cole and Tucker were little was negotiate obedience. I didn't have to yell. I didn't have to scream. And I certainly did not count! When I told my sons to do something, I expected them to do it. It didn't matter why. It didn't matter if they thought they should or shouldn't do it. It wasn't up to them. I wanted my boys to understand that Dad knows best how to take care of them. Sometimes they aren't going to understand my insistence on absolute obedience, but they need to trust my heart, because sometimes I can see what's coming around the corner.

A TRUE STORY

When Cole was about three years old, he was playing in the front yard. I had told him multiple times that he could never walk into the street unless Mom or Dad was with him.

I'll never forget the gleam in his eye the day he pushed the boundaries. I was doing something in the yard, and I looked up and saw him walking in the street—looking at me with a grin on his face. He knew better. This was a battle of the two wills: my will and his will.

Our neighborhood is really quiet. There's no through traffic—one way in, one way out. So if you are driving down our street, it's probably because you live there or are visiting someone who lives there.

Even though our street was quiet, Cole had intentionally crossed the line. And he knew it.

I took him inside, and we had a talk about obedience.

"Cole, why did you walk into the street?"

"But Dad, I didn't go far. I was right by the curb, really."

"I know, son, but that's not the point. I told you not to, but you did it anyway. You have to honor what Mom and Dad tell you to do."

I remember telling him specifically that he must *honor* what we tell him to do, whether he understands it or not.

And so I spanked Cole.

Tears flowed. He gathered himself and went to his room for a while to calm down. Life moved on as life always does.

THREE YEARS LATER

One day when Cole was six, I was in the yard working on something. (It sounds like I'm in the yard a lot, but I'm really not. I hate yard work—all of it.)

To the north of our yard there is a slight bend in the street. Not so much a tight curve, just a decent bend. If you're coming from the north, there's the bend first, then a stop sign, then our neighbor's yard, then ours. A few maple trees border our neighbor's yard, making it a little difficult to see very far past the bend or to see the stop sign.

Cole was about to cross the street in front of our home to go play with a buddy. By now, because he was such a responsible and obedient boy, and because our neighborhood was so quiet, we'd given him more freedom and had taught him to look both ways before crossing the street alone.

From the corner of my eye, I happened to see Cole stepping off the curb, about to cross the street right at the same time I heard the loud roar of an approaching vehicle.

I screamed—and I screamed only two words: *"Cole, stop!"*

Cole froze like a statue on the curbside. Literally. He locked up like he was on a remote control.

In that very moment, a teenage boy—I remember that he had brown hair—in a silver Pontiac Grand Prix came around the bend, blowing through the stop sign at what I conservatively estimated to be 45 mph in our sleepy little neighborhood. He was being chased by another boy in a green Nissan Frontier, who was going about 55, as they were horsing around and running stop signs.

They passed only six feet in front of my son's body, and they never even saw him. From the time I first heard the roar of the engine to the time I screamed, *"Cole, stop!"* was about seven seconds.

Seven seconds.

JASON CRUISE

Just thirty-six months prior to that horrific event, I had spanked my son because he had not obeyed. Yes, this time he had permission to look both ways and cross alone. He'd done everything right. He had more freedom because he'd earned it. Life, however, threw us the unexpected.

In that moment, it did not matter what Cole thought about my feelings of obedience. It didn't matter what he thought was fair or right or just. It didn't even matter that he had permission to cross the street at his own discretion. It only mattered that his dad told him to do something. I am convinced—*fully convinced*—that a spanking saved Cole's life that day.

And that spanking happened three years earlier.

There was no time to count, "One, two. . ."

There was no time to beg him, like I hear so many parents do these days in the aisle at the grocery store, "Son, please do what I said."

Three years earlier Cole had been taught by his daddy that he must trust his father's heart. Three years earlier he had been taught that if you don't obey, bad things can happen.

Obedience is nonnegotiable.

And obedience is always, *always* urgent (even when it doesn't feel urgent).

DISCIPLINE COMES DOWN TO AUTHORITY

Let me tell you where I stand: I want God's approval.

I want God's favor on my life and every inch of it. I want no area of my life creeping outside God's boundaries for me.

He is the authority, the kingmaker, the creator of the playbook. That means I couldn't care less about the approval of society at large. God created my sons, and therefore He is the authority on how they must be raised.

His Word tells me that I must "care enough" to discipline them. His Word tells me that I must not neglect them. He has counseled me to spank them for the betterment of their souls, and in some cases that protects them from speeding Pontiacs and Nissans, to keep them alive years later.

Loyalty to God matters to me so much that I honestly don't even think of loyalty to another.

You too must choose the authority to which you're going to be loyal.

#3
ESTABLISH THE PURSUIT OF HONOR

Establishing the pursuit of honor was on my heart from the very beginning as well.

Honor matters. And honor is a lost art these days. In fact, there was a time when honor was taught not just in the home but in the school system. Honor seems not to be taught anymore. Manners are requested or desired by teachers toward their students because being polite is nice, but even manners are really not demanded anymore.

When I was going to school, if a teacher felt like you were indignant or disrespectful, you'd never make it to the principal's office. You were taken into the hallway away from everyone's sight and paddled on the spot. Teachers weren't the only ones demanding honor. At my school the janitor would jerk a knot in you if you were out of line. And if you got in trouble at school, you were praying to holy God that someone from the school didn't call home and tell your parents. You'd get spanked at home for getting a spanking at school!

In those days the parent always sided with the teacher. Today parents always side with the kid, because, after all, their kid surely would never act up outside the parents' presence.

We have lost the ideal of honor.

STRANGE INVESTMENTS

It is strange to me, since we are talking about school thirty years ago and how school works today, that parents approach education so differently. Just as in the days when the Shema had much more communal influence than it apparently does today, schools were seemingly more formative a few decades ago in terms of character development.

Wendell Berry is perhaps one of the most influential writers in the past fifty years in America. He has an insane story of walking away from a stellar career as a writer and cultural influencer to go back to Kentucky to farm with mules when he could have used tractors. He went backward on purpose.

In his book *What Are People For?* Berry said:

> We think it ordinary to spend twelve or sixteen or twenty years of a person's life and many thousands of public dollars on "education"—and not a dime or a thought on character. Of course, it is preposterous to suppose that character could be cultivated by any sort of public program. Persons of character are not public products. They are made by local cultures, local responsibilities. That we have so few persons does not suggest that we ought to start character workshops in the schools. It does suggest that "up" may be the wrong direction.[4]

Following are some approaches I've used—with what appears to be a fair amount of success—to establish honor in my sons' character.

HONOR: WITH WORDS

> *Children, obey your parents in the Lord, for this is right.* HONOR YOUR FATHER AND MOTHER *(which is the first commandment with a promise),* SO THAT IT MAY BE WELL WITH YOU, AND THAT YOU MAY LIVE LONG ON THE EARTH.
> EPHESIANS 6:1–3

From the time Cole, and subsequently, Tucker, were young boys, I started right away working with them on the idea of honor. Please understand: honor is not the same thing as manners. Being nice and polite is fine, but manners must never be confused with honor.

Quite often my wife and I hear compliments from teachers or our friends that go something like, "Your boys have such great manners." Hearing that warms my heart. Nothing means more to parents than to know their kids are doing well navigating society. Yet I always find a way to include a little insight when receiving the compliment, because I believe it's a testament to biblical manhood.

My response is usually something like this: "Thank you so much. That means more to me than you know. I actually believe it's more than just being polite to you; I believe it's about honor. I want my sons to honor people, and that starts with honoring adults. Thank you for noticing."

It warms my heart when a boy, not just my boys but any boy, says, "Yes, sir," when talking to me. On the other hand, it breaks my heart to hear a boy say that with a broken spirit because he's been forced to say it.

I can hear his daddy say harshly, "Don't you say, 'yes,' to me, boy. You say, 'yes sir.'" That's forced. And honor cannot be forced. Honor must come from a desire to treat people with the honor they deserve as a soul created by God Himself. And that, friend, is far, far from good manners.

Teaching your son to honor souls with his words is not for the faint of heart. Teaching my boys took me about four years each. No kidding. From the time they could speak well, let's say eighteen to twenty-four months old, I consistently reinforced "yes, sir" and "yes, ma'am."

Our conversations would go like this:

> Me: Cole, do you like bananas?
> Cole: No, Daddy.
> Me *(with a smile and gentle tone)*: Make sure you say, "No, sir, Daddy."
> Cole: No, sir, Daddy.

He'd almost always repeat it back, which was awesome! And funny.

We used this gentle exchange for years before using "sir" and "ma'am" became ingrained in the fabric of their souls. You have to teach honor, and keep teaching honor, until your kids become unconsciously competent with it.

HONOR: WITH DOORS

The Bible speaks in many ways about love in action. The scriptures speak often of faith that has deeds to prove the faith exists. That means, at least in my estimation of biblical faith, that biblical words cannot carry much weight if they do not have the girth of biblical actions to follow them. Therefore, it is important to me that I find ways to model and teach honor in both word and deed to my sons.

Before either of my boys could walk, I taught them to open the door for their mama. I'd hold them in my arms as we'd walk up to a doorway, either at a store, or anywhere really, and as I'd open the door for Michelle, I'd say, "Okay, bud, let's open the door for Mama."

When you start when they are that small, they really have no memory of a time when they did not honor Mama. Their mother is the queen of the home, and a queen is worthy of honor.

I'll never forget when I knew I could stop reminding Cole to open the door for his mom, or for any woman. Cole and I had stopped to get gas. We were, in usual fashion, also planning to grab something to eat for the road. I wasn't paying attention all that much as we walked up to doors of the market, until I heard, "Oh, it's okay, honey, go on ahead."

What had happened was this lady had arrived at the door about the same time as Cole and opened the door for him. The problem was, he froze!

I looked up and saw him staring up at her as if to say, "Sweet lady, you're being so nice, but my daddy will have my hind end if I do this." The little fella was caught in both a societal and theological dilemma!

I started laughing and said, "Thank you. That's super sweet of you, but he's not about to walk in that door in front of you. That's why he's stuck! I don't think he's ever seen this."

She laughed too. And then she said, "My goodness. You just don't see that anymore."

As my boys grew older, I would let them fight the battle to get that heavy door open so Mama could get inside ahead of them. We'd walk up to a store or restaurant, and they'd pull just hard enough to get it barely open. Then they'd switch sides of the door by stepping inside the threshold so that they could push it open for her. It was the sweetest sight. I didn't help them because I wanted them to feel the weight of honor, to wrestle with the idea of honor.

HONOR: WITH HANDSHAKES

You can tell a lot about a man by his handshake.

A defining moment for me, when I knew something was out of whack in society, came in the form of a handshake. I was pastoring a church situated on a college campus. And we were reaching college students too, my man. It was super. We had them coming in droves.

I loved that part of the church's culture. I would work hard to stay in the students' lives, hang out with them, grab lunch, and do whatever I could to see them move forward in their faith journey.

It didn't take me long, however, to notice something about all of these young men who would speak to me before or after church. When they shook my hand, their grips were what I always imagined it was like trying to catch spaghetti: lifeless and limp.

On top of that, more often than not, they wouldn't look me in the eye if they did shake my hand. If they did look me in the eye, they'd almost never say their full name. These dudes were in great shape and good looking. Full of promise. They were men in the making, and the making was almost over.

I vowed then and there, based on my Sunday spaghetti experiences, that I would not assume that my sons knew anything about manhood, even down to how to shake a man's hand.

When each of my boys reached somewhere around the age of three, I would start teaching them how to shake a man's hand. The conversation would often go like this:

> Me *(with a smile and gentle tone)*: Okay bud, now we are about to go into this home. There's going to be people in there, and they are going to ask you, "What's your name, buddy?" or they will just start talking to you and ask you questions. When these people approach you, don't wait for them to stick out their hand. You beat them to it, okay? And remember, look them in the eye, speak up loudly so they can hear you, and make sure you say your full name.

That would take about thirty seconds, and I had to do it for years in the truck before we entered an establishment.

Tucker was hilarious when it came to this. He would tell them, with conviction and a serious tone in his little voice, "Hello, I'm Tucker David Cruise." He'd say it with a nod. It was awesome. (I had forgotten to tell him that the middle name wasn't necessary.)

Cole had his own way too. I've noticed that he, to this day, leans his head slightly left as he steps toward the person he is meeting, has a warm grin, and gives the greeting with a nod of his own. It's classic.

The whole name is important. It lets the stranger know you come from somewhere—that you have roots, and those roots tell a story of which you are both aware and proud. Anybody can be Cole. Anybody can be Tucker. There's only one Cole Cruise and there's only one Tucker David Cruise. And they have a story.

#4
USE MESSAGING

I love quotes. For whatever reason, quotes have forever stuck with me. I would say that the power of words just stays within me.

I cannot remember how I got the idea. I didn't read it in a book or hear about it anywhere, but some way, somehow, I came up with what we now creatively refer to in our home as "the chalkboard." Like I said, lots of creativity coming up with that moniker.

My goal was to get important truths in front of Cole and keep them there. I didn't put random, haphazard quotes or scriptures on the chalkboard. I put truth in front of him to undergird his DNA. This will make much more sense to you when you read what's coming about personality profiles for your boys; for now, just trust me when I say that I really wanted to head off what I saw as areas where Cole's personality would challenge him the most.

So I bought a piece of slate. Real slate, not imitation stuff from a discount store. I remember the day I climbed on eBay and found a 24-by-24-inch piece of slate for sale. It arrived at our home a few days later.

I cut the boards and then stained them after putting the frame together. I wanted time invested in the project, and I wanted Cole to see that by the investment of time, this chalkboard was not just some random thing. I could tell he sensed that this was no small thing. It's heavy, this chalkboard of ours.

I mounted it on the wall in his room. I then called him up there, and we had a discussion about influences and what goes into a man's mind. I told him that I wanted him to let certain truths about manhood resonate within his spirit. Therefore, I'd be putting these truths on the board from time to time. I told him there would be no test nor score to keep. I just wanted him to let these axioms soak into his bones.

Cole has an impressive work ethic, but in all honesty, it didn't come easy. When he was young, he would often take the path of least resistance. What kid doesn't, right?

But what Cole has, that I never had at his age, is discipline. He is a conformist, and he likes things to be locked down tight and ready. However, I noticed in his younger years, around the age of seven, he would make halfhearted attempts at cleaning up his room, or in his baseball practices, or even picking up after himself. And, while I most certainly was not going to allow a poor work ethic to get into his bones, I did not want to stay on him all the time with the heavy hand of a father.

I had to find another way to discipline him. . .without being a rigid disciplinarian.

Enter the idea of what we now refer to in our home as "The Chalkboard."

The first message I put on the chalkboard was this:

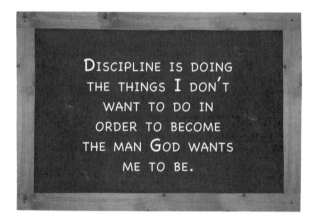

DISCIPLINE IS DOING THE THINGS I DON'T WANT TO DO IN ORDER TO BECOME THE MAN GOD WANTS ME TO BE.

At the time I'm writing this, Cole is now thirteen years old. And I can tell you this, he is absolutely not taking the path of least resistance any longer. He is one of the most prepared, focused, and joyful young men I've known; and I get to be his dad! Michelle and I often marvel at his work ethic.

That chalkboard worked. As simple as it was, it worked.

It kept the standard in front of him, without me having to

beat the drum of discipline at his every turn. Sometimes all it takes is slowing down long enough to be creative and finding a way to speak the language of your son.

TWO WEEKS

I didn't mention the chalkboard for at least two weeks. I hung it up, wrote down the first truth, and left it alone.

Driving down the road some two to three weeks later, out of the blue I said, "Hey, Cole, what is discipline?"

Without hesitation that boy said back to me, "Discipline is doing the things I don't want to do in order to become the man God wants me to be."

I almost cried.

It had worked.

I asked him, "So, you've been thinking about that?"

He said, "Yeah, Dad. I read it every day many times."

I knew the chalkboard was taking effect.

Remember that I told you that a plan doesn't have to be complex. A plan just has to be carried out. The chalkboard was my way of using truths and leveraging them against Cole's DNA. I knew he struggled with discipline, so I kept the truth in front of him in a way that was quiet and non-confrontational.

Here are a few other truths that have made their way onto the chalkboard:

Blessed is the man who does not walk in the counsel of the ungodly.

We used that one to talk about Cole's running buddies. We talk often about who he lets into his life, and why. Great leaders guard their influences because great leaders know they are able to be influenced. I want Cole to learn that now. He must learn that he's not impenetrable.

Fear is the thief of opportunity.

This one was monumental for chalkboard theology. Cole, by nature, can give in to his fears. He is plagued by the idea of making mistakes. On more than one occasion, while coaching his football team, I've had to call a time-out in the middle of a game and have his team take a water break while I confronted him about fear of failure.

I remember one specific game where we had a real heart-to-heart. I said, "You're killing your team because you're afraid to let them down. So you're frozen with fear, and what's that getting you? You've thrown three interceptions. . .because you're afraid to throw an interception!"

Cole is growing out of it slowly, but he battles fear of failure. And it does lock him up and render him ineffective at times.

This past baseball season there was a kid on the opposing team who was a twelve-year-old in a fifteen-year-old's body.

You've seen it before—the kid who is probably going to be seven feet tall when he arrives at college.

This kid stepped up to the plate, and he hit one of Cole's fastballs on a rope. As soon as it left the bat, I said to one of our coaches, "See ya." It was a boomer of a home run.

I walked out to the mound and told Cole exactly what my daddy told me when I was ten and gave up my first home run, "Son, good hitters hit good pitches. It was a great pitch, and he's a great hitter. You throw enough pitches and you'll have guys hit dingers on you occasionally. Now go have fun. It's part of the game."

The signage about fear stayed on Cole's chalkboard much longer than any other message did; I suppose that's because fear is such a demon for him right now.

OSMOSIS

The four Cruises were in the vehicle heading toward Virginia on a family vacation just a few weeks ago. We had just crossed the Virginia state line, as I recall.

The goal on this expedition was not the beach. We chose this particular year to try and mix family fun and national history into the vacation concept—which, as it turned out, wasn't so bad. We wanted our boys to experience colonial Jamestown and York-town, hoping they would understand the sacrifice it took to birth this nation called America.

Jamestown and Yorktown have worked hard to make history

interesting for kids. They have a lot of hands-on experiences—kids can grab a musket, use a piece of flint to skin hair off a tanning hide, or walk onto ships that are closely replicated to what our founders used to ferry them to our shores.

I cannot remember the context of the conversation while driving down the road, but somehow the idea of fear came up. I said to Cole, "And so, Cole, what is fear?"

Cole never had a chance to respond.

Tucker, age six, immediately interjected, "Fear is the thief of opportunity."

Michelle and I just stared at each other. Truth had made its way down the family tree. The power of the slate was exponential.

I suppose I shouldn't have been all that surprised at Tuck's declaration, for he'd obviously heard me coaching Cole on it at some point. Tucker, like any little brother, looks up to Cole with a holy admiration of sorts. Yet we were stunned at how the chalkboard had touched his life too. He'd read it. He'd interpreted it. He'd dealt with its presence.

Messaging works.

HIGH-TECH MESSAGING

We live in a world dominated by messaging. It seems silly even to speak it, for it is blatantly obvious. What is so different today, as opposed to the days when I was a boy, is that messages saturate life in more ways in our modern culture.

When I was a boy, you had billboards, magazine ads, television commercials, radio spots, mailers, and simple signage throughout the community—what today we call "traditional media."

As a parent, you couldn't control it, but you could get close to at least containing on some level what your son encountered or consumed. You didn't have quite so many creative streams running into the reservoir of your son's heart and mind.

Enter the smartphone.

Everywhere I go today I see ten-year-old boys with smartphones.

There's a term now that's employed by branding agents called "new media." It involves modern messaging vehicles, such as social media, texts, alerts, and ads coming across your phone's screen when you're reading a blog or some other media content.

STREAMING

Your son is a target market.

He always has been. I was a target market too, but as I said, messaging in the 1970s and 1980s was different.

Today messaging is almost unfiltered. There's so much of it, it's hard to contain. New media has crafted a culture that doesn't just include traditional forms like radio spots and magazine ads, but scores of mediums, such as Apple TV, Roku, YouTube, Snapchat, and on and on and on and on.

It's odd that we call it "streaming," don't you think?

All of these streams are now pouring into the reservoir of your son's mind and heart. Messaging is everywhere, and messaging matters.

THE POWER OF LOW-TECH MESSAGING

While the chalkboard may not be high-tech, the chalkboard works. Tucker's interjection that "fear is the thief of opportunity" taught me the power of the chalkboard.

That doesn't mean that Michelle and I go throughout our home writing scripture on the walls with Sharpies. I've seen a few parents do that, and it freaks me out a little.

Messaging does matter, so you must find a way to keep eternal truths about manhood in front of your son.

Your enemy has branding campaigns custom designed for your son, but your message is better. You must get it in front of him.

#5

CAPTURE COACHABLE MOMENTS

I try not to be lazy when coachable moments occur with my boys. It's not always easy, because sometimes I'm tired or just don't feel like coaching. However, I can think of few tools I've employed that have done more for my sons than coachable moments.

What I discovered about myself, and about most men, is that we assume too much. We assume that our sons are being taught good things in school. We assume that they know how to shake a hand. We assume that they know what a cutoff man is when playing baseball.

Yet if you step back and think about it, maybe your son was never taught what a cutoff man does when a ball is hit to the outfield. Your son has seen you shake hands, but he has never been told why it matters.

Refuse to parent by assumption.

When life hands you a moment, seize it. It won't take long—just a ninety-second conversation. And that ninety-second conversation will strengthen the foundation of your son's biblical manhood for years. So every time a coachable moment pops up, think of it as adding rebar to his mind and soul.

REFUSE TO PARENT BY ASSUMPTION

Here are a few real-life examples of how this has worked for me as a dad.

SCHLOTZSKY'S

From time to time we go to Schlotzsky's Deli for lunch after church. They make this one sandwich that I just love, and the boys seem to like eating there too.

On a recent trip, I was ordering a sandwich, and I asked the girl waiting on us to be sure that the preparers left the onions out of it. (I hate onions. The taste destroys a meal for me. Who knows why; it is what it is.) Upon the "no onions request," the girl said, "Well, sir, we can't do that. The onions are mixed in with the peppers in a prepared bag, and they come all mixed in together."

The "Hey, I grew up the son of a small-business owner" molecules of my DNA came to the surface fast. That was just the wrong answer. I, the customer, asked for something very simple. I was giving them my money. I chose to eat there. They should be happy about that!

The customer isn't always right. I learned that from watching my daddy at our hunting and fishing store: the customer will take advantage of you at times, so you must be careful.

However, that young lady couldn't convince me that taking onions out of a vegetable mix was an impossible feat. My response, and I promise you it was definitely kind and classy, was, "Well, it's not that you can't take the onions out. It's that you *won't* take them out."

She looked at me sort of funny and said, "Well, we just cannot do it."

I came back with, "No, honey, you can't convince me that your food preparers do not have the intellect to remove the onions. It's not that you can't do it; you won't do it. You refuse to do it. I'll take them off myself."

Cole and I sat down, and I began to talk with him about the exchange he'd just witnessed. It went something like this:

Me: Son, did you understand what I was telling

that lady? That it wasn't that they couldn't remove the onions; they just didn't want to take the time to do it.

Cole: Yes, sir, I could tell that was true.

Me: Son, let me ask you. What else do you see in this parking lot? Within 100 yards of where you're sitting, what do you see?

Cole: I see a McDonald's and a Macaroni Grill.

Me: That's right. So this isn't the only place to eat. We chose to eat here, and we chose not to eat there. And she's forgetting that. She's forgetting that Schlotzsky's isn't doing us a favor by serving us food. We are doing a favor for them by choosing to eat here. Customers pay her salary, not Schlotzsky's. I guarantee you that if you ask her who pays her paycheck, she'll say "Schlotzsky's," but that's not true. And do you know how I know that's not true? Watch what happens when customers stop walking through the door. Son, Sam Walton, the founder of Walmart, once said something to the effect that "there is only one boss: the customer. And he can fire everybody in the company from the chairman down, simply by spending his money somewhere else."

OH, THE IRONY

As I was smack in the middle of having this discourse with Cole about going the extra mile, the girl who took the order walked up to me. It turned out she was the manager on duty!

She said, "Sir, I figured it out. What I did was take off all the vegetables from your sandwich in the computer and resubmit the order with each vegetable listed separately. That way the onions are not premixed with the peppers, but each vegetable is a separate item. Then our chefs have to build it that way instead of using the premixed bag."

I was speechless. What a class act this young lady was, and how remarkable that it bothered her to the point that she was determined to figure it out.

COACHING 2.0

After the girl walked away, I knew the conversation had just been elevated to a whole new level.

I spent the next ten minutes talking with Cole about work ethic. We talked about finding solutions, not making excuses, and refusing to take the easy way out. Oh my goodness, was this situation tailor-made for a kid who, at times, can take the path of least resistance.

I told him that this young lady was a franchise owner's dream come true. She took it upon herself to do the work; and it wasn't about onions, it was about caring enough to solve a problem.

After our meal, I went to her, and we spoke for a while about the entire scenario. I told her that I was so proud of her—because it was never about onions. It was about treating others the way she would want to be treated. I told her she was a fine leader and that I was impressed by everything she'd done. And I made sure Cole stood by me to see and hear that too. It's critical that he see me handle things well *when things don't go well.*

Coachable moments require that you simply take the time to do the coaching. These moments are pure gold for you, Dad! Don't you dare let them escape.

Foundations matter. So put the rebar in your son's soul with every chance you get.

#6
PROVIDE CIRCLES OF MEN

I wanted to take Cole on a hunt with me and one of my closest friends. I know it doesn't sound like much at first glance, but in the kingdom of hunting, it's a monumental risk. Most men do not like to hunt with kids. It's just that simple.

Don't confuse that with the fact that a host of men love to take a kid hunting. When you do that, it's not the hunt you're after: it's time. When you hunt with a kid, you know the hunt is pretty much over before it starts. Kids get cold. They can't sit still. They need to pee at any given moment. So as a hunter, when you take a kid along, you have to recalibrate the gears in your mind.

When Cole was a little boy, I'd give myself pep talks before a hunt: "This isn't about hunting. It's about fun. It's about the giant dream in his head of seeing a huge buck. It's about the allure of the chase. It's about the snacks." All that mattered was that he had a good time.

CALLING CHAPMAN

This was different. I wanted Cole to see that his dad intentionally put himself around men of God. Sure, Cole had heard me preach that to him many times: "You must put yourself around kingdom men if you want to be a kingdom man."

There's an old preaching axiom, I think penned by Haddon Robinson, that says something like, "Why talk about it when you can show it?" In other words, preachers, don't talk about your chain saw in a sermon. Take that tool on the stage, crank up the Stihl, and let it eat!

I wanted Cole to see me interact with my closest circle. I wanted him to feel the vibe of being a young man around real men. And I knew that Steve Chapman would understand.

Steve is a Dove Award–winning musician, a widely known author, and a guy who desperately needs me to call up turkeys for him to kill.

Chapman is a true sage of the faith. So I figure that swapping time with a sage for my turkey-calling prowess and overall woodsmanship is a square deal.

Steve and I were scheduled to film a hunt for my Mossberg series, *The Rugged American Hunter*. I called him the night before and put him in a place, if I'm being completely transparent, where he really couldn't refuse the offer.

If a man asks you if he can take his son, and you get weird and squirrelly, you look bad. So all you can do is oblige and then go to your wife pouting about how this hunt is going to be a waste of time, and you can't believe that somebody would do this to you—and on and on and on you go.

Chapman is different. He knows how to raise kids, and he's written about it often. And he's sung about it even more. When I called him, I said, "Look man, I've got a favor to ask. Obviously, you're the one killing the bird tomorrow. I've been talking to Cole lately about the kind of people he lets into his life, and I want him to see me modeling that. So how about if he comes along?

"Steve, I promise you, man, he's a good hunter. He's still. He's quiet. He doesn't get cold easily. And there's no way he's bringing a gun. You're killing the bird. He's already killed two this year anyway. I want him to see that his dad intentionally pursues time with men who are further down the road of faith."

And so Chapman was fine with it. At least by his tone. I knew he was thinking exactly what I'd be thinking in terms of a kid not blowing the hunt: *Yeah, we'll see about that.*

DOUBLING DOWN ON THE EXPERIMENT

Chapman handled the hunt like the sage he is, in all his glory. He took time with Cole, talking with him, not just with me. He let him set out the decoys. He was perfect.

We laughed, ate snacks, made jokes, talked about life and marriage and work. That is about as routine of a hunt as any Chapman and I have ever been on in the past.

At about 8:30 we finally got a tom to commit. This bird entered a low-cut clover field from about 300 yards away, and I hit him with some savvy yelps. He went into strut immediately. The tom then proceeded to walk right at us, stopping only for a few seconds to strut and walk; it was as if he had read the script.

I gave Chapman the green light, and the bird went on to glory. Chapman, ever the wordsmith, looked over at me laughing and said, "The boss bird met the Mossberg." I think he'd been crafting that one for a while, but I didn't ask.

UNEXPECTED

As we were sitting there drinking in the remaining adrenaline, smoke still coming out of the gun barrel, I looked up and another tom had entered the field almost exactly where the first one had five minutes before. The wind was blowing quite well that morning, and I think the sound of the shotgun blast was somewhat muffled. I let out three silky yelps, and this bird did the exact same thing—headed toward us like he was on a rope. Strutting. Gobbling. And beautiful. Fanned out against that solid green wheat and clover. It was nothing short of gorgeous.

Chapman eased me his vintage Mossberg 835, and I ended up shooting this bird, almost piling him up on top of the first one.

I turned to Cole and said, "Son, you've seen the hunt of a lifetime."

We still talk about it today.

WHY THIS MATTERS

This was more than a hunt. We showed Cole manhood instead of talking about it. Cole heard us talking about marriage. He felt the weight of discussions about money and pending work projects. He had to put himself in a position of submission too. Most guys want the kid to take the shot if the shot comes, and Chapman most certainly tried to get me to do the same. I wanted Cole to watch and learn. I wanted him to observe, and observe he did.

In today's world, kids are protected—as they should be. We

shield them from all sorts of things. And we should shield them and protect their innocence as long as possible. However, my sons have to learn how to carry themselves around men. They have to learn how to talk and when not to talk in a circle of men. They have to learn their place in the process of growing up. These are things they cannot get from playdates and Little League baseball.

I've never shielded my boys from circles of men who can model for them how to act, talk, and think like a man. I've had to teach them how to interact with men. To shake hands. To laugh. To listen. To be in a mind-set where they are not the center of attention, nor do anything to bring attention to themselves as a kid; if they do that, they won't be asked back in most cases.

I can talk to my sons about manhood, but why talk about it when you can show it?

#7
KEEP A MANHOOD JOURNAL

Keeping a manhood journal may be the coolest thing I've ever done. The longer I live, the more I see that a man doesn't have that many cool ideas, so this may be my one cool idea!

I started writing in high school, and my work was first published in high school. I suppose I've forever had a love for writing. Once you see your work in print, it does something to you.

I want my sons at least to try their hand at writing, for I

believe the world needs—in fact, depends on, in many cases—good writers. In a world where texting and emojis rule the day, I fear that twenty years from now if there exists a man or woman who can spell properly, complete a sentence, and do all of that on paper, they just might win the Pulitzer Prize.

And thus came the idea of the manhood journal. Several years ago I had the thought that maybe, just maybe, I could get Cole to write down his thoughts about what it takes to be a man.

LEATHER

There's something about good leather.

I'm not a fan of black leather. However, I'm a sucker for brown saddle leather. Good, worn, brown hide with a story behind every crease. Yeah, that's just about heaven for me in the form of a book bag, shoes, wallet. Even my iPad cover is first-class leather.

I had my favorite preaching Bible covered years ago in English cowhide. It's like something you'd find in Spurgeon's collection; it looks amazing. Stereotypical though it may be, leather is a milepost of manhood in my estimation.

I thought that it might be neat if Cole could journal about manhood—his thoughts, not mine. And so we hopped in the truck one day and journeyed off to a bookstore where we picked out a fine leather journal. I played up the experience. I sat him down and told him our reason for being there.

"Cole, I want you to start writing down your thoughts about

what it means to be a man and what it means to be a man of God. I think it'll be good for you to write, especially since school is out for the summer."

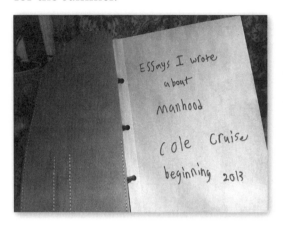

Cole gave me a deep and well-thought-out response: "Okay."

I was hoping for more. Something Hemingwayesque, but I settled for the one-word answer and left it at that.

OF TRUCKS AND THEOLOGY

It took me a week or so to decide how I was going to execute this wonderfully cool journal idea of mine. My biggest concern was that Cole wasn't coached. I wanted his words about manhood to travel through his own filters, even though at the time he was only eight years old.

I recall the conversation very clearly for some reason. We were driving down the highway, and I said, "Hey, buddy, you know we bought that journal last week. I want you to start thinking about what it means to be a man, but I don't want you to write down what you think I think about manhood. I want this to be your thoughts, okay?

"So let me ask you, Cole, when you think about the qualities of being a man, what are they? What does it mean to be a real man of God?"

I was in no way prepared for how he'd respond.

Cole said, "Well, Dad, I think a real man is loyal."

Taken aback by the depth of his answer, I came back with, "Okay, that's great. Tell me what you mean. Explain it a little more."

Cole explained, "I think loyalty matters. I think a real man is loyal and never leaves his friends stranded."

That's an eight-year-old boy talking.

I didn't know what to say. I was stunned at how he had not come at me with some short answer like, "A real man goes to church." That's the sort of stuff you'd expect, because that is what a Christian kid should say!

On that ride home, I knew that Cole's first journal entry would be about loyalty.

MAKING THE JOURNAL WORK

It's true that I didn't want the manhood journal to be forced. I wanted it to be original—from Cole's heart. However, there was one area where I did want to move his thoughts from being a real man—to focusing on being a real man who loves God.

I came up with this three-phase model. Let's use the loyalty idea as the framework.

1. Define loyalty.
2. Give an example of loyalty.
3. How is God loyal to me?

The one thing I discovered was not to expect a page per topic! Cole would most always write one sentence, maybe two if I was lucky. That was acceptable, because the goal was to get him to think through his thoughts.

The real test was in getting Cole to connect the idea at hand to the heart of God. In the case of loyalty, I wanted Cole to see how God had been loyal to him.

It was, and still is, important to me that he not just pick out character traits of manhood that are absent of God's eternal heart. I wanted Cole to see how God was his authority for manhood, and I more deeply wanted him to see that his desire to be loyal originated with the God who loves him.

WHAT COLE DOESN'T KNOW

Cole will probably write five essays a year in the manhood journal. *Essays* is a strong word. It's more like *sentences*.

As he's getting older, I can see a few more words appearing in the topics he chooses to write about, and it's neat to watch his writing develop. He's putting more thought into his journaling—most of the time anyway.

If I took away anything from Robert Lewis's classic work

Raising a Modern-Day Knight, it was his passion for "rites of passage," the ceremonies that launch a young man into manhood. Lewis argued that ceremonies are a "plumb line" moving a young boy through the mile markers of manhood.[5] I'd agree. The power of ceremony is monumental.

Ceremonies lock things into our minds. We can go back to them. I remember the key rites of passage in my life clearly. My first car and the day I got my license. My baptism. My graduations. My ordination. My wedding. These were all ceremonial. And thus the memory is clear and powerful.

My plan is that when Cole is around eighteen years old, I'll quietly stop having him write about manhood. I'll let the journal ease out of his memory, but you can be sure I won't have forgotten about it.

I'll either do it on the night before his wedding or the night before his graduation—I can't decide which, but it will be one of those two highly esteemed occasions. A circle of people will be gathered around him—grandparents, friends, girlfriend or fiancée. He will be just about to launch fully into manhood. The night will be lit with excitement and accolades. Everyone dear to him will be there, celebrating him as a grown young man. The future will be bright with promise, and I'll have the floor for a few moments. In that moment, I'll pull out the journal and present him with the book he wrote, starting when he was eight years old, on what it means to be a man.

#8

PERSONALITY HARDWIRING:
AMERICA'S BIGGEST PROBLEM WITH CAREER PATHS

America has a massive problem with preparing teenagers for career paths. Truthfully, I've not seen much change in my lifetime in this arena, and yet we have more resources than ever before in terms of coming alongside teens to steer them toward fulfilling careers.

How can I say that I've not seen much change, having done absolutely no research to back my findings? Easy. Really, really easy. Just ask a teenager who is approaching eighteen years of age, "What do you want to do for a career?"

The conversation will go much like this, for I've asked this question many times. (Yes, it comes across as being a total joy killer at first. Nevertheless, it works.)

Me: What do you want to do for a career?

Teen: I want to be a doctor.

Me: Why?

Teen: I think it's neat to help people who are sick. And you make great money.

Me: Yeah, it is really neat. So, how do you feel about working sixty to seventy hours a week? That's roughly twelve hours a day. I can tell you love being outside; you talk about how much you love to camp, to be active in nature. Do you realize that you'll be indoors all the time? Like all day, every day. You'll make a ton of money! You won't get a lot of time to spend it. Do you know that you like dealing with sick people? Have you ever thought about what it's like to only deal with sick people all the time? How are you going to pay for it? Do you realize that you'll graduate with close to $200,000 worth of debt immediately staring you in the face? Mainly, do you know God has called you to be a doctor? Have you asked Him about your calling?"

Teen: (*Blank stare. No response.*)

When I say that I know—*that I know*—our education system, our communities, and our churches are doing very little to launch our next generations into career paths, it's because I'm getting the exact same answers my friends and I gave when we were asked the same questions in the 1980s.

To be clear, I never leave my conversations with teenagers on that note of killing their dreams in a small, shallow moment! I talk with them at length about their DNA and how they can find a life of joy if they will only change how they are thinking about life and career and calling.

DNA

In my years after college while pursuing my master's work, I began to realize just how severe the failure was of parents, communities, schools, and churches to prepare kids for a fulfilling career. I was determined to change that when I had children.

One of my main goals in raising Cole and Tucker is that they attend their high school graduation with a thorough understanding of how God made them, where they are gifted, and where they are weak.

Americans are obsessed with being balanced. Balance is a myth. Balance isn't even biblical.

Take time to read these verses carefully. Paul is talking about spiritual gifts and how a person puts them into use.

> *And He gave* some *as apostles, and* some *as prophets, and* some *as evangelists, and* some *as pastors and teachers, for the equipping of the saints for the work of service, to the* building up of the body *of Christ; until we all attain to the unity of the faith, and of the knowledge of the Son of God, to a mature man, to the measure of the stature which belongs to the fullness of Christ.* As a result, *we are no longer to be children,* tossed here and there *by waves and carried about by every wind of doctrine, by the trickery of men, by craftiness in deceitful scheming; but speaking the truth in love, we are to grow up in all aspects into Him who is the head, even Christ,*

*from whom the whole body, being fitted and held together
by what every joint supplies, according to the proper
working of each individual part, causes the growth of the
body for the building up of itself in love.*
EPHESIANS 4:11–16, EMPHASIS ADDED

The scriptures are clear that God gives *some* to carry a role, but he doesn't give every person every gift. Balance just isn't biblical.

Writing to a group of new Christians in a town called Ephesus, Paul is talking about spiritual living in a pagan culture. Paul is taking great strides to make sure the believers aren't deceived by strange theology in this society that didn't value Christianity.

I realize that this letter to the Ephesians is not about raising kids. It is, however, about what happens when you don't know your gifting! When you don't know your gifts, you'll find it hard to attain maturity, and unity in the church will suffer. When you don't know your gifts and how God has hardwired you, you get tossed around in confusion.

Great leaders spend huge amounts of energy learning who they are, and they spend the same energy learning who they are not.

Balance is a myth.

REPORT CARDS

So your son comes home with four As, two Bs, and one D. What's the conversation about almost immediately?

The D.

Never mind that your son just scored eight out of ten overall. As parents, we are manic about our kids being perceived as weak in any one area.

Maybe for your son, the D he received in biology is really an A+ in that field of study. Maybe he just isn't science minded. Maybe he has a teacher who has a whacked-out way of teaching science.

Have you ever compared his other science scores across time to the D he just received in biology? Is there a trend across the years?

Let me ask you, right now in your established career, if you're an introverted mechanical engineer or an introverted financial analyst who loves data, spreadsheets, metrics, key performance indicators, and operational processes, how you would feel if your boss told you that you were in danger of losing your job if you didn't immediately attain an A+ level at public speaking and sales.

That's right. Sales.

You are now expected to support your salary with your ability to sell the product of your company. Revenue is weak, and you have to start selling. And that means knocking on doors of potential clients. Your boss also gave you a call sheet and a list of hot leads. The boss then told you, "Now, get on it. Go meet people and make friends and bring home some revenue growth."

You'd panic! Your stress level would go through the roof immediately.

And you'd start putting together a résumé—quickly—because you want out of there as fast as possible; the demands are completely unrealistic.

THE LIE OF EQUALITY

Have you ever seen Michael Jordan play basketball? God did not create us all as equals.

Have you ever seen a PGA tour professional hit a 2 iron? I have. Many times. My dad was a professional golfer.

I remember the first time we attended the Masters Tournament in Augusta, Georgia. I was fourteen years old.

My favorite time of attending Augusta was sitting at the range watching legends like Nick Faldo, Fred Couples, Ernie Els, and Steve Jones hit balls. I remember telling my dad, "They hit their 2 iron as straight and consistently as I do an 8 iron."

I knew then that my chances for making "the tour" were fading. Fast!

God did not create us as equals in terms of talent. And when Michelle and I had children, I was determined to make sure that my sons knew who they were—and who they were not.

My sons are as different from one another as you could possibly imagine. This is my favorite image of them. It tells you everything you need to know about them.

One is calm and collected.

One is a party searching for a place to happen.

They are created differently, and they are hardwired differently. Therefore I dare not parent them with the same template.

JETS FOOTBALL

When my boys were around the age of seven, I started teaching them that they were not good at everything. It was important that they not fall into the trap of that deception.

Take a look at this image.

That's my son Cole at quarterback. At the time he was ten. The center is a boy named Ty. Cole and Ty have been playing ball together since they were five years old.

Now look closer at the tailback—the one with his hands on his knees. That's Abraham. He goes by AJ. I've been coaching AJ since he was five years old as well. AJ is a freak of nature.

At the age of five, when he carried the ball, AJ reminded me of Barry Sanders of the Detroit Lions. Sanders was basically the inventor of what is now known as the "jump cut." Sanders wouldn't just juke a defender; he was so quick and light on his feet that he'd stop while running at full speed by landing on both feet and bounce like a rabbit in the other direction. His moves were stunning to watch. Defenders would be left standing still, as if to say, "What just happened?"

AJ ran like Barry Sanders. In fact, I had to come down on AJ for playing games with defenders. The interaction was hilarious. AJ was almost impossible to catch, especially in the formative years of U5 to U8 when most kids weren't as football aware as AJ was. He knew how to run the ball and was ahead of his age group in carrying the ball down the field. He would jump cut and break free, and after he'd get a 10-yard lead in the open field, he'd slow down!

He'd grin at defenders with his green mouthpiece and let them catch up so that he could juke them again! How cool is that? He loved the cat and mouse game because he knew he was both the cat and the mouse.

I remember talking to him during halftime at one game when he was about seven years old. With a smile on my face, I said, "Hey, look, dude, when you break free, go ahead and score, okay? It's not cool to embarrass them twice!"

We laughed, and he said, "Okay, Coach."

He knew I'd caught on to his game.

THROWING AIN'T RUNNING

Cole isn't a fast runner. He came by his speed honestly because I'm slow too. I was slow when I was ten, and I'm slow now. At about the seven-year-old mark, Cole was beginning to talk about how he felt embarrassed because he wasn't fast like some kids. It was the first time we talked about gifting in any depth. I knew I had the perfect example that would make the most sense to him: I had AJ.

The conversation went about like this on the way home from practice one night:

> Cole: Dad, I'm just not fast.
>
> Me: (I could tell it was really bothering him) Cole, you and I both know that AJ is fast. Really, really fast. And agile. He moves left to right as good as anyone you'll ever encounter. I don't think I could catch AJ. However, have you even seen AJ throw a football?
>
> Cole: Well, yes sir. He's not bad.

Me: That's right, son. He's not bad at all, but you are more accurate than he is at quarterback. Now, you can't run like AJ. My word, I can't run like AJ; but you can't measure your ability to run with speed like AJ—and AJ can't measure his ability to be accurate like you. God made you both different for a reason. And you have to accept it, because that's how God makes a team work together. Right now, if you tried to match his skills, you'd struggle. If he tried to match your skills, he might struggle, too.

I believe the conversation about comparison was a defining moment for Cole. And now I find myself having those very same conversations with Tucker.

Tucker is such a strong young man. I believe Tucker is going to be an amazing Kingdom leader. He has a fierce, warrior heart, filled with joy and energy. Yet, there are times now as he's growing up that I see the same dragons haunt him over comparison.

Comparison is one of the most lethal toxins a man can have, and it lives in all of us. The conversation about AJ is the type of conversation we have often in our home. Comparison is not God's best for us, because it sets us up for failure on so many levels.

One of the biggest challenges I had as a youth football coach was getting young boys to learn to play a role. I led many devotions after practices based on Romans 12:4–5:

For just as we have many members in one body and all the members do not have the same function, so we, who are many, are one body in Christ, and individually members one of another.

I would constantly tell the boys that it takes every man on the field for one guy to score. And it was something I had to teach them time and time again.

DNA IS ON YOU, DAD

It's up to you, Dad, to teach your sons that balance is a myth. And the sooner you teach them that God has given them a specific hardwiring, the faster they'll learn to play from strength instead of weakness.

You can find several tools for exploring gifting: Strengths-Finder, DiSC Personality Profile, Enneagram tests, and a wide variety of online spiritual gift tests. You have more tools than ever before to help your sons discover how God made them unique.

Imagine how differently the conversation about career path possibilities might go once you use some of these tools with your son. Suppose I approach your son and begin the following conversation:

Me: What do you want to do for your career?
Teen: I want to be in the medical field. Not sure

specifically just yet, but I want to be in medicine.

Me: Why?

Teen: God has gifted me with healing and mercy. These are spiritual gifts listed in the scriptures in 1 Corinthians 12:10 and Romans 12:1–8. Every time I do spiritual gift tests, I rank high in mercy and healing, and I believe God can heal by speaking it Himself; but He can also heal through doctors called to use medicine. I've also been on a few mission trips, and I feel the hand of God on me when I'm ministering to sick people.

Imagine how different our culture would look if young men and women knew that college may not be their best choice. College is a waste of time, talent, and money for many people.

Imagine the world without plumbers and electricians. Imagine the world without roofers. Imagine the world without musicians. Imagine the world without sculptors. Imagine the world without truck drivers. Imagine the world without farmers.

So why demand that your kid go to college when he doesn't even know what he wants to be? And why demand your kid go to college when you haven't done anything to help him figure out how God hardwired him?

When a man knows who he is—and who he is not—he knows what to say no to and not feel guilty about it. I want my sons to play from strength, for I know it's the path to fulfillment.

I want them to know that God's hand is present on their lives and callings. And I will make sure that when they are asked by an adult, "What do you want to do with your life?" that they'll have biblical framework fueling their answer.

7

AN UNEXPECTED WITNESS

Parents are unprepared for a ton of things when it comes to raising children. As I said in the beginning of this book, there's no playbook guaranteeing great kids. It seems silly to even say that out loud, for all parents know how true it is.

I remember the days when Michelle was pregnant with Cole. A constant voice in my head seemed to say, "Are you prepared for this?" Now I can say with absolute clarity, "No way was I prepared, and I'm still not prepared."

Many times I felt the weight of not knowing exactly what to do. And of all the areas where I felt the weight of the unexpected, this one perhaps surprised me most. It started to take form when Cole was around two years old and seemed to happen almost always at restaurants. Michelle and I would be sitting there, with Cole in a booster, happily engaging life as new parents. Just a typical family eating lunch like any other family would. Nothing special about that at all.

Inevitably, a man and woman would be on their way out of the eatery, and they'd stop by our table. The conversation usually went like this:

> Stranger: Hey, excuse me. I hate to interrupt your meal, but we've been watching your son.
> [Okay, so right there we went into sheer panic. We'd stop listening to what they were saying for a second because the movie in our heads started playing back. *What did he do? What did I not do? Did he steal something? Did he eat something off the floor? Were we arguing too loud and forgot that we were in public? Did he pee on the floor and we didn't see it happen?* These were the thoughts that exploded in our minds.]
> Me: Oh boy. Did he do something?
> Stranger: No. We just couldn't get over how he was acting. He didn't throw food. He wasn't loud. We even heard him say, "Yes, sir." There's order here and there's peace. And he's so little. How did you do that?

No kidding, sometimes people would even ask us if we'd been reading a book on raising kids, and if so, they wanted to know the title!

What usually happened next in those conversations with strangers taught me about the power of God working through parenting. I'll confess, I never thought about the power of God working through me as a parent. I was familiar with God working through me as a leader. A writer. A preacher. A speaker. That sort of stuff made sense. I just never thought of parenting as a conduit of God's glory to the world around me.

REVERSE EVANGELISM

The first few times strangers approached us, Michelle and I graciously took the compliment and thanked them. However, after several repeat encounters, we realized these were opportunities to talk to strangers, people we'd never meet again, about our faith.

It was like evangelism, but in reverse. We started to take a gospel approach to these meetings. After all, people were approaching us; we weren't approaching them. The unexpected aspect was that I never dreamed that we'd be able to talk about Jesus because of how we were parenting. We weren't practicing some parenting model. We were just trying to bring Cole up with discipline and honor in some of the simple things, because he was only two years old.

Actually, we were raising Cole with a biblical worldview handed down to us by our parents. We were doing what came naturally to us. So it wasn't like we were necessarily aware of the moves we were making. We believed in the scriptures, and we were simply ensuring that Cole had the discipline he needed to know life's boundaries.

From the time Cole was two until the time he was six, I'd

say we were approached by inquiring strangers at least twenty-five times. Although the encounters were odd, we got used to them. They didn't just happen at restaurants. We'd find ourselves fielding questions from teachers, neighbors, or strangers at ball games where our sons would be with us in public. Time and again people would ask us, "What did you do to get them to behave that way?"

It was in those moments that this book was being written in my heart. As a dad, I was practicing what I was preaching. And I was noticing that other parents were starving for answers. And that's what I want to make sure you don't miss: we weren't stellar parents who had all the answers.

THE PTERODACTYL

Would you believe that I honestly thought about titling this book *The Pterodactyl*? You know about that dinosaur, don't you? The ancient, weird bird with the crazy-shaped head. The reason for my potentially unusual title was because everyone has heard of a pterodactyl, but no one has ever seen one.

What is true of the pterodactyl is too often true of boys in today's culture. One rarely finds boys who have honor, class, and unyielding conviction. Boys who own biblical values. Boys who shake hands with purpose in their voice and life in their eyes. Boys who know how to treat a young lady with honor on their first date in high school. Strangers were approaching Michelle and I to ask about our parenting because boys like ours are like pterodactyls in our eroding culture—nearly extinct.

I see pterodactyls from time to time, so I know they are out there, but they are rare birds. I believe parents were approaching us about our boys and the order that our family seemed to have because it was something they'd heard was possible but maybe didn't believe could really happen for them too.

Many parents we'd encounter were exhausted from failed attempts at raising their kids to listen and obey. We could see stress and defeat all over their countenances. We could see their fatigue from dealing with what was now a teenage daughter who had become unbearable and just plain hateful in how she spoke to her mother. Grandparents would approach us with broken hearts over how their grown children were allowing their new grandchildren to live seemingly without boundaries, which was so far from how the grandparents had raised their kids who were now in the trenches of parenting.

Almost always I'd start my response with something like this: "Thank you. It's very kind of you to talk with us. You asked, and so I'll tell you. We believe that the God who created the child has the right to tell us how to raise the child. We believe that it's more than manners—it's honor. The Word of God tells us that children are to honor their mother and father. And so we are doing our best to raise our son according to the Word of God. That goes both ways. We have biblical expectations of him, and we have biblical expectations of ourselves too. God is the authority, and we are walking according to His Word on how to raise kids."

RISKY, VERY RISKY

Don't think I'm not aware of what's going on right now.

You have no idea how vulnerable I feel sharing that story about strangers approaching us over the class and honor with which our boys have been living in today's culture. You and I both know that every meal didn't turn out that way. There were times it was just the opposite! There were times, especially at Cracker Barrel, when things didn't go well.

For some reason, Cole went through this epic love/hate drama-filled relationship with Cracker Barrel. We talk about it to this very day. It began about the time he was eighteen months old and lasted for about six months.

All was right with the world. . .until they brought out the biscuits and corn bread just before the meal.

About 50 percent of the time we'd visit Cracker Barrel during that six-month window, that little, joy-filled, orderly pterodactyl would become a T. rex. Nasty. Foul. Crying. He'd throw a diva fit. We had no idea why. We'd stop it quickly, and on a few occasions, I'd have to take him outside and get him to compose himself. It was strange.

So, yes, you and I both know that sometimes things just unravel on you when you're in the trenches of daily life.

Michelle and I both know that we are far, far from perfect in our ability to raise kids. However, that doesn't mean we aren't doing some things right. Kids change as they become adults. Sometimes you do everything right and kids still take the road of everything wrong. We've all seen that happen, and it's tragic. Nevertheless, I won't back down from talking about my sons, for they do in fact make me very proud. They are far from perfect, but they are stellar young men. You too can raise stellar young men as you fully commit to it on every level every day.

I never knew just how much the world was watching—and how they were watching as hungry souls looking for answers to finding peace in the home. I never anticipated that working to cultivate peace in our home would be a conduit for talking to other parents about the Prince of Peace who could bring peace to their homes.

8

IN THE THICK OF IT

As I write this book, I'm sitting in my little office. John Coltrane is playing quietly in the distance, like a soundtrack to a morning that hopefully stays normal. I like a little jazz when I write. Don't know why, but I do. Life is going fine at the moment.

We have football practice tonight. I just got a text from Michelle, and we're trying to figure out who is picking up whom. We have two practices in fact. I coach Tucker's team at 5:15 p.m. and then Cole's team at 6:15 p.m. When practice is over, we'll grab something to eat on the way home.

Homework will be required. That'll be dramatic; you can bet on that. There will be lamenting and gnashing of teeth and complaining about how tired they are from working so hard at practice, and how that fatigue justifies more downtime to do what they want to do, which is anything but homework.

Before or after homework there will be showers.

Then the real drama will go down: getting them into bed.

To this very day, I have no psychological or theological understanding as to why the idea of going to bed is utterly catastrophic to their souls. You'd think we were discussing amputating their toes without any anesthetic.

And it happens every single night. *For years! Every year, every day!* Seriously. We go through this same stupid emotional loop around bedtime every evening.

As I write this book, I'm in the thick of it.

Just like you are.

I really struggled on what to title this project because it's a risky venture. I'm very aware of what writing a book about parenting says to the world around me. I chose to title it *In the Thick of It* because nothing is closer to the truth. I'm navigating parenting daily.

Cole is entering a new journey of manhood.

He's in the front stages of puberty. And that means I'm literally thinking through how to improve my game and meet the demands of being a dad with a son in the middle of a perpetual testosterone attack.

And just last Tuesday night, out of nowhere and completely unannounced, Tucker gave up Nite Nite, his stuffed toy dog. My heart absolutely broke as I made my way down our wooden staircase. The tobacco-colored hardwood felt like quicksand under my feet

as I went down each step. I walked into our bedroom where Michelle was folding clothes and said, "Tucker just told me, 'Dad, I don't need Nite Nite. You can put him in the closet.'" Neither of us could speak. We just stood there staring at one another through glassy eyes. We knew what was happening.

We have but a moment with our children. The days seem long and drawn out, but the years are fast and brutally ruthless with their quick passing. So we must get it right. We cannot afford to get it wrong.

You and I must choose sides. Because raising boys will straight kill a man if he isn't sure of where his loyalty lies.

> *"Choose for yourselves today whom you will serve. . .but as for me and my house, we will serve the LORD."*
> JOSHUA 24:15

NOTES

Chapter 1: Divided Loyalties

1. Robert Frost, "The Road Less Traveled," PoemHunter. com, accessed April 4, 2018, www.poemhunter.com/poem/ the-road-not-taken.

Chapter 4: Culture and Plumb Lines

1. Gordon MacRae, "In the Absence of Fathers: A Story of Elephants and Men," LinkedIn, July 10, 2015, www.linkedin.com/ pulse/absence-fathers-story-elephants-men-gordon-j-macrae.

2. "The Delinquents of Pilanesberg," The KOTA Foundation, accessed April 4, 2018, www.kotafoundation.org/ the-delinquents-in-pilanesberg/.

3. Robert Lewis, *Raising a Modern-Day Knight: A Father's Role in Guiding His Son to Authentic Manhood* (Carol Stream, IL: Tyndale, 1997), 15, emphasis added.

4. Ibid., 65.

5. William Kilpatrick, *Why Johnny Can't Tell Right from Wrong* (New York: Simon & Schuster, 1992), 252.

Chapter 6: Sowing Manhood

1. Robert Lewis, *Raising a Modern-Day Knight: A Father's Role*

in Guiding His Son to Authentic Manhood (Carol Stream, IL: Tyndale, 1997).

2. Albert Einstein Quotes, Goodreads, accessed April 4, 2018, www.goodreads.com/quotes/search?utf8=%E2%9C%93&q=If+you+-can%27t+explain+it&commit=Search.

3. James Dobson, *Bringing Up Boys* (Wheaton, IL: Tyndale, 2001), 228–29.

4. Wendell Berry, *What Are People For? Essays* (Berkeley, CA: Counterpoint, 1990), 26.

5. Robert Lewis, *Raising a Modern-Day Knight: A Father's Role in Guiding His Son to Authentic Manhood* (Carol Stream, IL: Tyndale, 1997), 114.